CLASSROOMS IN MOTION

USING LEARNING STATIONS FOR HIGH STUDENT ENGAGEMENT IN GRADES K–5

SAMANTHA K. DYKES
RACHEL E. MORRIS
SHANNA K. HELMKE

Solution Tree | Press

Copyright © 2025 by Solution Tree Press

Materials appearing here are copyrighted. With one exception, all rights are reserved. Readers may reproduce only those pages marked "Reproducible." Otherwise, no part of this book may be reproduced or transmitted in any form or by any means (electronic, photocopying, recording, or otherwise) without prior written permission of the publisher.

555 North Morton Street
Bloomington, IN 47404
800.733.6786 (toll free) / 812.336.7700
FAX: 812.336.7790

email: info@SolutionTree.com
SolutionTree.com

Visit **go.SolutionTree.com/instruction** to download the free reproducibles in this book.

Printed in the United States of America

Library of Congress Cataloging-in-Publication Data

Names: Dykes, Samantha K., author. | Morris, Rachel E. (Teacher) author. | Helmke, Shanna K., author.
Title: Classrooms in motion : using learning stations for high student engagement in grades K-5 / Samantha K. Dykes, Rachel E. Morris, Shanna K. Helmke.
Description: Bloomington, IN : Solution Tree Press, [2025] | Includes bibliographical references and index.
Identifiers: LCCN 2024033991 (print) | LCCN 2024033992 (ebook) | ISBN 9781960574961 (paperback) | ISBN 9781960574978 (ebook)
Subjects: LCSH: Classroom learning centers--United States. | Student-centered learning--United States. | Education, Elementary--Activity programs--United States.
Classification: LCC LB3044.82 .D95 2025 (print) | LCC LB3044.82 (ebook) | DDC 372.13--dc23/eng/20241009
LC record available at https://lccn.loc.gov/2024033991
LC ebook record available at https://lccn.loc.gov/2024033992

Solution Tree
Jeffrey C. Jones, CEO
Edmund M. Ackerman, President

Solution Tree Press
President and Publisher: Douglas M. Rife
Associate Publishers: Todd Brakke and Kendra Slayton
Editorial Director: Laurel Hecker
Art Director: Rian Anderson
Copy Chief: Jessi Finn
Proofreader: Jessica Starr
Text and Cover Designer: Fabiana Cochran
Acquisitions Editors: Carol Collins and Hilary Goff
Content Development Specialist: Amy Rubenstein
Associate Editors: Sarah Ludwig and Elijah Oates
Editorial Assistant: Madison Chartier

Acknowledgments

We would like to extend our heartfelt gratitude to our former principal, Carol O'Donnell, for always believing in us and giving us the opportunities to try our innovative ideas. Your unwavering support and encouragement have been instrumental in our journeys, and for that, we are forever grateful. Thank you to Dan Ludwig for continuing to support us over the past few years; we appreciate you helping our vision become reality.

We are thankful to Nathan Wear for bringing us into the Solution Tree family. Your belief in our vision and your continuous support have made this endeavor possible. We are honored to be part of such an inspiring community.

To the teachers who have taken a leap of faith with us and implemented our framework into their classrooms, we extend our sincerest thanks. Your willingness to embrace new ideas and your dedication to enhancing student learning have been the driving forces behind the success of this framework. Your courage and commitment inspire us every day.

Lastly, to our family members, thank you for your endless support and understanding throughout this process. Your patience, love, and encouragement allowed us to pursue our passion with confidence and dedication.

With sincere appreciation,

Samantha, Rachel, and Shanna

Solution Tree Press would like to thank the following reviewers:

Tonya Alexander
English Teacher (NBCT)
Owego Free Academy
Owego, New York

John D. Ewald
Education Consultant
Frederick, Maryland

Janet Gilbert
Principal
Mountain Shadows Elementary School
Glendale, Arizona

Shanna Martin
Middle School Teacher & Instructional Coach
School District of Lomira
Lomira, Wisconsin

Lauren Smith
Assistant Director of Elementary Learning
Noblesville Schools
Noblesville, Indiana

Visit **go.SolutionTree.com/instruction** to download the free reproducibles in this book.

Table of Contents

Reproducibles are in italics.

About the Authors vii
Introduction 1
    Why We Need Engagement in the Classroom 3
    The Student-Engaged Framework 4
    What You Will Learn in This Book 8

Part 1 – Foundations 11

Chapter 1: Communication, Accountability, and Relationships 13
    Teacher Self-Awareness Check 14
    The Role of Communication 15
    The Role of Accountability 26
    The Role of Relationships 38
    Conclusion 48

Chapter 2: Personalized Learning Tools 49
    Teacher Self-Awareness Check 50
    Personalized Learning Environments 52
    Self-Management and Student Agency 60
    Conclusion 66

Part 2 – Learning Stations.................................. 69

Chapter 3: Minilesson Station........................... 71
  Teacher Self-Awareness Check............................. 73
  Understanding the Minilesson Station..................... 74
  Implementing Minilessons................................. 77
  Conclusion... 89

Chapter 4: Independent Work Station..................... 91
  Teacher Self-Awareness Check............................. 92
  Understanding the Independent Work Station............... 94
  Implementing Independent Activities...................... 98
  Conclusion.. 107

Chapter 5: Collaboration Station....................... 109
  Teacher Self-Awareness Check............................ 110
  Understanding the Collaboration Station................. 112
  Implementing Collaborative Activities................... 115
  Conclusion.. 121

Chapter 6: Digital Content Station..................... 123
  Teacher Self-Awareness Check............................ 124
  Understanding the Digital Content Station............... 126
  Implementing Digital Activities......................... 129
  Conclusion.. 135

Epilogue.. 139
Appendix.. 141
  Implementation Guide.................................... 141
  Practice Unit for Kindergarten Through Second Grade..... 147
  Practice Unit for Third Grade Through Fifth Grade....... 151
  Check, Check, Done! Checklist Template................ 153
References and Resources.................................. 155
Index... 165

About the Authors

Samantha K. Dykes, an instructional coach in the Linn-Mar Community School District in Marion, Iowa, has been a driving force in inspiring innovation through professional development. Her educational journey began in 2011, and she has since taught grades K–5 English learners, grades 6–9 English learners, and grades 3–4 general education. She served as an online learning coach during the 2020–2021 school year.

Samantha's passion for education extends to higher learning institutions. She has taught both undergraduate and graduate courses on literacy and English learning at Coe College and the University of Dubuque in Iowa. Her expertise has also been shared at local and national conferences, where she presents innovative strategies for effective classroom practices. Her educational philosophy aligns with the axiom that the whole purpose of school is not to be good at school but to be good at life. This drives her commitment to engage students and equip them with essential skills for beyond the classroom. The student-engaged classroom model that she champions serves as the foundation for her teaching beliefs.

Samantha is not only an educator but also an active community member supporting youth initiatives in Linn County, Iowa. Additionally, she contributed to Connections, an online resource for English learners by Perfection Learning.

Samantha's educational path began at Iowa State University, where she majored in elementary education and received her K–12 English as a second language endorsement. She has also earned master's degrees in English learners and learning and technology from Western Governors University and a master's degree in administration with a principal endorsement from Northwestern College in Orange City, Iowa.

Rachel E. Morris is an instructional coach in the Linn-Mar Community School District in Marion, Iowa. Throughout her years in education, beginning in 2006, Rachel has continually demonstrated her unwavering commitment to student success and staff growth. Starting as a grades 4–5 classroom teacher, she honed her skills in curriculum design, classroom management, and student engagement, serving on numerous curriculum and leadership committees throughout her district. Driven by her passion for helping others thrive, Rachel transitioned into the role of an instructional coach, supporting teachers and providing them with the tools, resources, and guidance they need to excel in their practice. Her expertise in instructional strategies, data analysis, and collaborative problem solving has empowered educators to enhance their teaching practices and improve student outcomes.

Rachel is an avid advocate for lifelong learning and community engagement. She actively participates in professional development workshops, has presented at state and national conferences, and partners with Marion Cares, a local nonprofit organization in Marion, Iowa, to serve youth and families in the area who are underprivileged.

Rachel received a bachelor's degree in elementary education from Wartburg College in Waverly, Iowa, and both a master's degree in elementary reading and mathematics from Walden University in Minneapolis, Minnesota, and curriculum and instruction from Western Governors University. She is currently working toward a master's degree in administration and a principal endorsement from Northwestern College in Orange City, Iowa.

About the Authors

Shanna K. Helmke has been a dedicated educator since 2011. She currently serves as an instructional coach in the Linn-Mar Community School District in Marion, Iowa, bringing a wealth of knowledge and expertise to her role. Her journey in education began in the elementary classroom, where she taught grades 3–5, focusing on student engagement and innovative teaching strategies. Alongside her work as an instructional coach, Shanna also serves as an adjunct professor at Mount Mercy University in Cedar Rapids, Iowa, furthering her commitment to fostering excellence in education.

Throughout her career, Shanna has been recognized for her outstanding contributions to education. Her expertise has been popular at various conferences, where she has presented on topics such as technology integration, blended learning, and innovative teaching methods. Shanna is trained in cognitive coaching and adaptive schools, equipping her with skills to support and empower educators in their professional growth. As a Seesaw for Schools Ambassador, she advocates for the effective use of digital tools to enhance student learning experiences. Shanna's dedication to continuous improvement is evident in her pursuit of professional development in areas such as blended learning, Universal Design for Learning (UDL), and the leveraging of technology in the classroom.

Shanna's educational journey began at the University of Iowa, where she earned her bachelor's degree in elementary education with a minor in psychology and endorsements in early childhood, reading, and social studies. Building on this foundation, she pursued advanced degrees, including a master of education in learning and technology and a master of science in curriculum and instruction from Western Governors University, and a master of education in administration with a principal endorsement from Northwestern College in Orange City, Iowa. These qualifications have equipped Shanna with the knowledge and skills to lead and inspire educators toward success.

To book Samantha K. Dykes, Rachel E. Morris, or Shanna K. Helmke for professional development, contact pd@SolutionTree.com.

Introduction

When you enter Miss Furlong's classroom, you immediately notice visual supports accessible to all students. Visual aids include student work expectations, schedules, and learning goals, promoting self-sufficiency and providing a sense of structure and purpose to the students' learning.

A digital timer ticks down; students are responsible for efficiently managing their work time and understanding self-management as they navigate four learning stations: (1) the minilesson station, (2) the independent work station, (3) the collaboration station, and (4) the digital content station. The organization of the four stations caters to the learners' various learning styles and preferences. Students are engaged in their work because they have voice and choice as they meet their learning objectives and have autonomy throughout the learning process.

Students rely on one another for support as they can work independently and collaborate with their peers while the teacher engages a small group of students to focus on explicit, direct instruction without distractions. Having students rely on each other and collaborate promotes a positive classroom culture that creates a sense of community and cooperation. This is possible because the teacher has implemented a framework that has empowered self-reliant, resourceful students who obtain a sense of ownership over their education.

The skills the students learn from this well-organized and student-focused learning approach prepare them for their continued education and beyond.

We stand at an intersection of tradition and progress, where a traditional classroom no longer meets the needs of the students, and classrooms must adapt to prepare students to thrive in an ever-changing world. The traditional classroom (of what we call the *factual era*) was set up in a way for students to learn and repeat facts. During this factual era, people would seek out fact holders in a specific field to gain knowledge from them; for example, they would visit local experts, read specialized books, or attend lectures. Google, among others, disrupted this era by making it possible for anyone with a smart device to access factual information in minutes. Therefore, students no longer needed to be fact regurgitators. Eric Sheninger (2021), author of *Disruptive Thinking in Our Classrooms: Preparing Learners for Their Future*, states that the changing work world "requires a new way of doing school. A business-as-usual model based on efficiency, repetition, and knowledge acquisition will only prepare students for a world that no longer exists" (p. 7). Teachers can no longer provide students with the facts they need to succeed at a specific job because the jobs they will have as adults may not exist yet.

Research from McKinsey & Company shows that to be successful beyond the classroom, students need cognitive, interpersonal, self-leadership, and digital skills (Dondi, Klier, Panier, & Schubert, 2021). The skills include thinking critically, communicating effectively, having mental flexibility, developing relationships, working effectively with others, being self-aware and goal oriented, and having digital fluency and citizenship skills.

For students to develop these real-world skills, their engagement in the classroom is essential. Across all grade levels and content areas, academic research supports a strong correlation between student engagement and achievement (Lei, Cui, & Zhou, 2018), showing that it directly impacts motivation, comprehension, and retention. By understanding why engagement matters, educators can better appreciate its role in fostering a dynamic and effective classroom environment. In the following sections, we explore the significance of engagement and how it transforms the learning experience and introduce a comprehensive framework designed to achieve high levels of student engagement. This framework provides practical strategies and tools that teachers can implement to create an all-inclusive, interactive, and stimulating learning environment. Throughout this book, you will learn how to effectively apply these strategies, tailoring them to your unique classroom needs to maximize student participation and success.

Why We Need Engagement in the Classroom

Classroom engagement is generally defined as students' active participation in the learning task or activity. Engaging students is a constant battle marked by rapid technological advancements. Eric Sheninger and Thomas C. Murray (2017) state, "This 'Netflix generation' of students (and all future generations) has no basis for understanding information that is not readily and immediately available. These students have come to expect high-quality content on demand, anytime, anywhere" (p. 59). Because of technological advancements, students have adapted to expect instant gratification and rapid information, which conflict with traditional school instruction.

Student engagement can encompass various components, such as movement, empowerment, and relationships. It can also involve factors like purpose, motivation, commitment, voice, and choice. However, movement, empowerment, and relationships are essential elements that often contribute significantly to engagement in the classroom. Let's look at each.

- *Movement* in the context of engagement refers to students' mobility in the classroom and active participation in the content through talking while standing or moving, engaging in hands-on activities, and collaborating on projects. Using manipulatives to concretely understand a mathematical concept and tapping the sounds they hear in a word are ways students can physically connect with the content they are learning. Movement is a way to engage students' brains. Stephanie Knight (2017), doctor of educational leadership and professor at Grand Canyon University, explains the impact of movement, stating that a simple two-minute burst of movement every ten minutes (think of activities like *stand up, pair up* or *walk, pair, share*, or just simple stretching exercises) can induce reactions in students' brains that help them retain learning and increase their levels of focus and engagement.

- *Empowerment* in the classroom involves giving students the authority, autonomy, and resources they need to make decisions, take control of their learning, and positively influence their classroom environment. Empowered individuals feel a sense of ownership and responsibility, which fosters their engagement and motivation to effect change. This component is about enabling students to have voice and choice in their learning to drive change in their lives in and out of the classroom. In their book *Empower: What Happens When Students Own Their Learning,*

John Spencer and A. J. Juliani (2017) say teachers needn't change the entire system to provide a different student experience.

- *Relationships* are a fundamental component of engagement. Building and nurturing meaningful relationships with others can be highly motivating and create a sense of belonging and community. Positive relationships within the school setting lead to increased engagement. Whether the relationships are with peers, adults, or oneself, these connections play a significant role in shaping one's level of engagement. Forming a relationship within oneself and forming relationships with others are equally important as mental health needs are on the rise.

In particular, let's consider this last point about relationships. According to the National Center for Education Statistics (2022):

> Sixty-nine percent of public schools reported an increase in the percentage of their students seeking mental health services at school since the start of the COVID-19 pandemic, and roughly three-quarters (76 percent) of schools also reported an increase in staff voicing concerns about their students exhibiting symptoms such as depression, anxiety, and trauma.

If students feel confident in themselves and understand their value and worth, it can help combat the mental health crisis.

As a teacher, and given these realities, you might wonder how you can create an equitable and effective learning environment that allows students to have autonomy, build strong relationships, develop life skills, and authentically engage in relevant learning. As the next section details, we have a framework for doing just that.

The Student-Engaged Framework

The *student-engaged framework* described in this book can reshape any classroom, engage students, empower them to drive their learning, and prepare them for an unknown future. This specific framework provides multiple advantages to both the teacher and the student. It provides a clear structure throughout the classroom, instructional consistency, and a strong focus on learning outcomes, and it encourages collaboration among content areas. Students benefit from increased clarity and predictability, logical progression of learning through a variety of facets, and improved self-assessment with goal setting.

Introduction

To create a clear structure within the classroom, the student-engaged framework is broken into four stations that students work through: (1) the minilesson station, (2) the independent work station, (3) the collaboration station, and (4) the digital content station. The four stations provide opportunities for students to complete tasks requiring decision making, problem solving, memory, attention, and judgment—all of which rapidly increase student learning. Each station can take anywhere from ten to twenty minutes, depending on the tasks assigned and the students' age. Older students (grades 4–5) can focus their attention and remain engaged for longer amounts of time than younger students (grades K–3). Station times are also dependent on the amount of time teachers have allotted in their daily schedule. All these variables factor into the amount of time scheduled for each learning station. The beauty of the student-engaged framework is the flexibility it offers to accommodate learners' and teachers' schedules.

Through a synthesis of meta-analyses depicting what influences work best in education, John Hattie (2023) finds that the average effect size of all the interventions he studied is 0.40, which represents the hinge point of positive and negative effect sizes. Any influence that scores higher than 0.40 has a positive effect on student learning, and anything that scores lower has a negative, detrimental effect on student learning. According to Hattie (2023):

> The major question for educators is to know thy impact, which begs questions about what impact means. At a minimum, this impact refers to educating students to know that, know how, and know with. This emphasis on the right balance of surface, deep, and transfer knowing and thinking requires critical judgments, appropriate teaching, optimal learning strategies, and appropriate assessment. Educators need to be explicit about what they want their students to know, do, and care about. (p. 44)

Based on Hattie's (2015) research related to student achievement, cognitive task analysis—which teaches students how to think about content and focuses on the preceding traits of decision making, problem solving, and so on *in addition to* the content—has an effect size of 1.29, meaning it has a highly positive impact on student achievement.

While the chapters throughout the book engage at a deeper level with station implementation, let's take a quick, high-level look at the stations and how they facilitate students in cognitive task analysis.

1. **Minilesson station:** During this station, the teacher meets with small groups of students, typically ranging from three to six students,

depending on their individual needs for direct, focused instruction. The station is designed to provide targeted support to students who may need additional help with a particular skill or concept or to challenge students who are ready for more advanced work. The minilessons are carefully planned to align with academic standards and address specific student needs. By meeting with small groups in the minilesson station, the teacher provides personalized and differentiated instruction while fostering a sense of connection and support among the students in the group.

2. **Independent work station:** During this station, students engage in purposeful practice of previously taught skills, work on challenging tasks, or receive reteaching to reinforce learning. The station is designed to connect academic standards and include a variety of materials and resources to support the learning objectives. For example, the station might include fluency passages, workbook pages, writing practice, Seesaw activities (https://seesaw.com), a QR code hunt, and so on, allowing students to practice and reinforce key skills.

3. **Collaboration station:** This is a dynamic and interactive learning station where students work together on hands-on activities that promote peer-to-peer collaboration, communication, creativity, critical thinking, and decision making. This station encourages students to work collaboratively to solve problems, conduct research, create projects, and much more. For example, students might work together to build a covered wagon from teacher- or kit-provided materials or create a play discussing how people used their covered wagon to travel the Oregon Trail. The collaboration station needs to have clear guidelines and expectations for working together, such as taking turns, listening to others, and respecting different perspectives. This station helps foster social-emotional skills while supporting the development of academic knowledge and skills.

4. **Digital content station:** In the digital content station, students engage in purposeful practice with digital resources and tools. The content is carefully selected to align with academic standards and support the learning objectives of the class. This station is a balance between independent learning and collaborative learning. Independent learning at this station needs to be purposeful and differentiated for each student. In this case, use technology to gather data on student performance related to standards, and tailor learning experiences to meet the needs of each individual student. These data,

collected through various educational software and tools, such as Seesaw, Freckle (https://freckle.com), and Quizizz (https://quizizz.com), help teachers identify each student's strengths and areas for improvement, list specific skills students need, and allow for more tailored and effective instruction. Collaborative learning at this station sees students work together to further their learning using digital tools and modes of communication. Examples include group research projects, collaborative gameplay using Osmo (www.playosmo.com), and group discussion through the use of breakout rooms on a conference platform like Zoom (https://zoom.com). At this station, teachers seek to strike a balance between students' collaborative use of technology and use of it in isolation to learn.

To enable students to navigate their stations and stay on track, our framework has teachers use a *Check, Check, Done!* checklist that includes a comprehensive list of all the activities available at each station. The checklist, which you'll learn more about in this book, has checkboxes next to each activity, and students mark off each task as they complete it. This provides a clear visual guide for the students to follow and fosters a sense of responsibility and accountability as they track their progress. The Check, Check, Done! checklist helps students effectively manage their time and ensures they engage in purposeful learning at each station. The checklist also serves as a useful communication tool among teachers, students, and families. Teachers can use the checklist to quickly assess each student's progress and then send it home to give parents insight into the learning that took place.

To meet all students' needs during their stations, an individualized Check, Check, Done! checklist can provide modifications and accommodations for individual learners. Classroom teachers can create these checklists on their own, with another colleague who also supports their students, or with grade-level teams when applicable. For example, the classroom teacher can collaborate with the English learner teacher to create a Check, Check, Done! checklist for a student that includes independent practice on a speaking standard. Classroom teachers can reinforce practice for students in the mainstream classroom during the independent work station due to collaboration with specialty teachers. Teachers can also work together as a team to divide and conquer, creating the Check, Check, Done! checklist, sharing it with other classrooms, and making small tweaks if needed for their own classrooms.

The student-engaged framework also features embedded components of personalized learning, including opportunities to individualize and personalize learning through a checklist, along with the essential principles of Universal Design for Learning (UDL), such as student voice and choice. This makes the framework something that teachers can implement with confidence, knowing research-based strategies back it. Cornell University's (n.d.) Center for Teaching Innovation highlights the value of UDL as:

> a teaching approach that works to accommodate the needs and abilities of all learners and eliminates unnecessary hurdles in the learning process. This means developing a flexible learning environment in which information is presented in multiple ways, students engage in learning in a variety of ways, and students are provided options when demonstrating their learning.

By implementing four learning stations and building these necessary skills that prepare students to be college and career ready, the student-engaged framework meets all students where they are in their learning journey. As you dive deeper into this book, you will learn about not only why we created this framework but exactly how you can implement it so your students can benefit from a classroom that empowers students and teachers.

What You Will Learn in This Book

The purpose of this book is to offer you systems, structures, and routines to implement in your classroom to authentically engage students and positively impact learning. Authentic engagement entails rigorous, challenging work that is relevant to students' lives. An authentically engaged classroom fosters relationships, builds trust among students, and offers a space where every student belongs. The student-engaged framework can be implemented in any K–5 classroom, and its components are adaptable for any content area.

To make the most of this framework, a strategically designed classroom environment is critical for creating routines, visuals, engaging activities, and systems that are appropriate for the task and purpose, meet the needs of all students, and increase movement. Learning environments will be designed to give students autonomy in how they want to learn, voice and choice to pick the path and pace for their learning, and daily practice to implement executive functioning skills. Through intentionally designed learning stations, students are challenged at their level and drive their learning to become active creators of knowledge.

This book will support your transformational journey to implementing the student-engaged framework through two parts: (1) foundations and

(2) learning stations. Part 1, "Foundations," includes the foundational elements needed for the learning stations in part 2 to function effectively. It includes the following two chapters.

- Chapter 1 defines verbal, nonverbal, and visual communication. We create systems within systems in the classroom as students learn accountability for themselves and their learning through the development of strong relationships.
- Chapter 2 introduces student self-management tools, including the Check, Check, Done! checklist, and it shows how to use the learning environment itself to personalize learning and empower students with voice and choice.

Part 2, "Learning Stations," includes in-depth learning of each learning station. It consists of the following four chapters.

- Chapter 3 describes how to implement a minilesson station that provides effective direct instruction in your classroom for small groups of students. The chapter shares strategies for grouping students, differentiating instruction, and measuring learning through assessment.
- Chapter 4 focuses on how to structure an independent work station. You will learn how to plan individualized instruction by collaborating with support or specialized teachers to provide accommodations and modifications that meet students' individual needs and skills, and can be reinforced in the mainstream classroom.
- Chapter 5 emphasizes teaching students how to interdependently collaborate in a collaboration station. The chapter includes examples of projects, games, and other interactive experiences to foster communication, critical thinking, and teamwork among students, and it shares resources that you can adapt for your own classroom collaboration station.
- Chapter 6 showcases how digital content and tools can and should be used in a digital content station. Standards and content will be supported with digital resources that are highly motivating and engaging.

Like the introduction to this book, each chapter begins with a classroom scenario. This is followed by a teacher self-awareness check that invites you to reflect on your current practices through a series of thought-provoking questions. These questions encourage you to examine your teaching approach, classroom environments, and student interactions. By delving into your current approach, you will gain a deeper understanding of your strengths and areas for improvement. This reflective approach fosters a sense of ownership and self-awareness, empowering you to make meaningful changes that enhance student engagement and learning outcomes in your own classroom. Each chapter also provides background information, an explanation of why the learning station is important, and implementation strategies. We include examples and visuals throughout.

By the end of this book, you will restructure your classroom to authentically engage your students. This book is a tool you can pick up, read, and apply one step at a time at your own pace. We show you all the parts and pieces of the framework throughout the chapters, and in the appendix, we provide a four-week structure that puts them all together. A couple of practice units—a penguin unit tailored for grades K–2 and a solar system unit for grades 3–5—are also provided, as well as a blank Check, Check, Done! checklist template. You can follow the implementation path we've laid out or utilize the given templates to implement any procedures or structures you see fit for your classroom learning environment.

Implementing a student-engaged classroom is a process, not a program, and is reflected through our four guiding principles.

1. We believe that all students should be challenged at their level and recognize their worth and potential.
2. We believe that the whole point of school should be not to make students good at school but to prepare students to be good at life.
3. We believe that the teacher is the facilitator of the learning. With the right tools and systems in place, students should drive their learning.
4. We believe that student engagement positively influences academic growth by focusing student learning through the foundational pillars of relationships, empowerment, and movement.

As fellow educators, we are excited for you to embark on this journey of implementing the student-engaged framework in your classroom. Enjoy learning about the foundations of our framework and the research that supports it. We hope that you find the tools, templates, and resources helpful as you engage in implementing learning stations and that you see your students respond to learning in a more efficient and engaging way.

PART 1

FOUNDATIONS

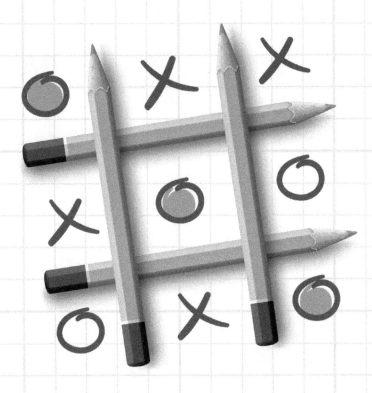

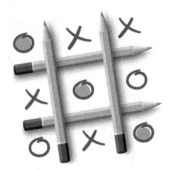

CHAPTER 1
COMMUNICATION, ACCOUNTABILITY, AND RELATIONSHIPS

During small-group stations in Ms. Eagle's classroom, Matthew, a quiet student, has just returned from reading support. He sees classmates working together. Some are reading independently, a couple are on their laptops, and the teacher has a group of students at the back table. Matthew has no idea what to do on entering the classroom; he knows not to interrupt the teacher while she is in a small group and can't think of anyone else to ask. He quietly takes his seat at his desk and waits for the teacher to finish with her group and give the class further directions.

Kira, another student, has just moved from Guatemala. She misses her old friends, her old school, and her old neighborhood, where everyone spoke her native Spanish language. Once a top student in her fifth-grade class, she now feels her classmates see her as dumb because they don't understand her.

Brayden, a student with autism, has a challenging time communicating with his peers. He often expresses himself through his body language and communicates with noises. Because peers have not had the opportunity to interact with Brayden, they are often distracted by Brayden and don't know how to respond when this happens and interrupts their learning.

This scenario describes students and situations that can occur in any classroom. Although these students face different challenges, they all need the same things: clearly communicated procedures, learning expectations, and the opportunity to connect and form relationships within the classroom. These things are all necessary in operating an effective learning environment. In this chapter, we will discuss the importance of implementing strong communication, holding students accountable, and building positive school relationships in order to support the student-engaged framework.

Teacher Self-Awareness Check

To begin your exploration of this topic, use the questions in this section to examine your teaching approach, classroom environments, and student interactions. Through this reflection, honestly observe your own strengths and areas for improvement as you seek to make meaningful changes to enhance student engagement and learning outcomes in your classroom. (Visit **go.SolutionTree.com /instruction** to access reproducible versions of Teacher Self-Awareness Check sections in this book.)

Which students seem lost or confused about what they should be doing during your school day?

_____
_____
_____
_____
_____

Are there times in your schedule that you find students wandering the room, sitting compliantly at their desks, or needing several reminders to stay on task?

_____
_____
_____
_____
_____

How many of these students know what to do when they don't have clear instructions from you?

_____
_____
_____
_____
_____

Which students in your class have a tough time connecting with others?

_____
_____
_____
_____
_____

We have all experienced students who seem lost, are unable to navigate the classroom, and don't know how to transition to their next learning task. Clear behavior and learning expectations will help guide them. Some students may wander or distract peers because they are unsure of the work they are supposed to be doing. Having accountable practices present can keep them focused. Others don't have a strong sense of belonging in the classroom and may feel isolated. Implementing practices for positive relationships can help. All these things can occur daily within a classroom and reiterate the need for clearly communicated expectations and systems that hold students accountable for their learning and behavior and ensure every student feels valued as part of their learning community.

The Role of Communication

As teachers, we constantly communicate with our students, greeting and welcoming them, reiterating a procedure, correcting behavior, explaining a mathematical process, dictating words for students to encode, fluently reading a passage, or answering student questions. As things we do with automaticity every day, the many daily opportunities we have to talk and interact with the students in our classrooms are easy to take for granted. But these are also times when you build healthy and productive relationships with students and engage them with learning. As Stevenson University (2023) writes:

> As humans, we are drawn to one another and communicate with each other in a variety of capacities. There are several roles that each individual fills on a daily basis, depending on the context of an interaction. What every interaction has in common is the need for clear and effective communication.

Consider also the words of Douglas Fisher, Nancy Frey, and John Hattie (2016), who write, "The ways in which teachers consciously and subconsciously communicate their expectations to students are too numerous to list. Expectations are everywhere, in every exchange teachers and students have" (p. 17). For example, think about how we communicate about teacher and student roles and the need for teachers to provide clear behavior expectations and procedures so the classroom can operate effectively. These expectations should be posted so that anyone who walks into the room is aware of them and students can refer to them anytime they need a reminder.

Teachers' use of concise, effective language to communicate learning targets is also imperative for students to understand learning expectations. Aligning learning targets to standards and explaining proficiency prepare students for success with the learning objectives. If teachers do not clearly communicate these key pieces of information, students will not have a purpose for learning, affecting their motivation and engagement. Learning must be relevant to motivate students.

Students also have a communication role in the student-engaged framework—understanding the rules, procedures, and behavior expectations set for them. They are responsible for following the expectations, acting accordingly, and learning the academic content. If they are confused by or misunderstand expectations, they need to be taught how to advocate and ask questions. When teachers establish clear behavior and learning expectations, students can navigate the classroom on their own, liberating the teacher to focus on instruction and be undeterred by disruptions or distractions.

In the following sections, we examine some ways that communication often breaks down in the classroom and how you can implement more effective communication practices.

UNDERSTANDING HOW COMMUNICATION BREAKS DOWN

Communication happens in infinite ways, so there are also infinite ways for that communication to break down. For example, without clear procedures, teachers experience interruptions in learning due to student misunderstandings or lack of adherence to rules. Whether students act out because they don't know what is expected of them, cause disturbances because they aren't equipped with the skills necessary to complete a task, or simply ask questions because they don't understand, all these behaviors cause instruction to stop so the teacher can redirect students and get everyone back on track. This redirection takes precious time away from learning, and these disruptions add up over time. Matthew Kraft (2020), associate professor of education and economics at Brown University, states:

> Small interruptions and the disruptions they cause can add up to a considerable amount of lost learning time. Drawing on our detailed observation records, we estimate that approximately three and half minutes of instructional time is lost due to interruptions each hour of the school day. Teachers' estimates of time lost are even higher, at almost six and half minutes per hour. Scaling these estimates by 5.5 hours per day and 180 school days per year suggests that students lose between 10 to 20 days of instructional time over the course of the year. (p. 33)

Further, constant daily reminders can also be exhausting, and teachers often find themselves sounding like broken records, repeating directions and expectations.

Something else to consider in the complex classroom system is the emotional state of students and how our communication can impact them. All humans have an emotional bank account, which is based on trust and how comfortable they feel with another person. Just as a literal bank account depends on your withdrawals and deposits of money, all interactions can result in positive deposits into your emotional bank account or negative withdrawals. Think of these as the ratio of positive comments students hear from you relative to any negative comments they receive (no matter how constructively they're intended). According to leadership consultants Jack Zenger and Joseph Folkman (2013), in the research rooted in business studies, "The average ratio for the highest-performing teams [is] 5.6 (that is, nearly six positive comments for every negative one)." According to Kyle Benson (2017) with the Gottman Institute, studies on happy marriages indicate that ratio is five positive interactions to counteract one negative. Sean Covey (2014), the international best-selling author of *The 7 Habits of Highly Effective Teens*, supports this research when he refers to an emotional bank account as a relationship bank account, stating:

> In a checking account, ten bucks is ten bucks. In [a relationship bank account], deposits and withdrawals are not created equally. It usually takes many deposits to make up for one withdrawal. One subtle but demeaning comment . . . can destroy weeks of deposits. (p. 133)

It doesn't matter what the context is; researchers agree a high ratio of more positive than negative interactions between two people is best to have an effective, healthy relationship.

In the classroom, withdrawals from teachers are inevitable throughout a school day. Placing verbal demands on students, asking questions, repeating directions, and correcting students represent withdrawals from their emotional bank accounts. Although there are specific times when teachers need to redirect and command students within the classroom, it is important to remain conscious of students' emotional bank accounts. Removing unnecessary withdrawals and replacing them with tools that empower students can be an effective way to maintain a positive ratio within teacher-student interactions.

Finally, communication overload and cognitive overload should be avoided within the classroom. The American Psychological Association defines *communication overload* as "a condition in which more information is presented to a person . . . than can be processed or otherwise effectively utilized by the person" (Communication overload, 2018). Further, the American Psychological Association defines *cognitive overload* as "the situation in which the demands placed on a person by mental work (the cognitive load) are greater than the person's mental abilities can cope with" (Cognitive overload, 2018).

Our brains can handle only so much information in our working memories, a topic about which instruction expert Julia A. Simms (2025) writes extensively in *Where Learning Happens: Leveraging Working Memory and Attention in the Classroom*. This is why, for example, it's hard to follow directions with more than three or four steps without rereading them or referring to the given information. Fred Jones and Patrick Jones (2023), creator and authors of the Tools for Teaching classroom management strategies, explain a solution to cognitive overload when they talk about visual instruction plans. In the verbal modality, we hit cognitive overload within a few sentences. That is hardly enough explanation to produce clarity with a complex concept or operation. Instead, teachers "must replace verbal prompts with visual prompts to create clarity while reducing the duration of the interaction" and "reduce the verbosity that creates cognitive overload" (Jones & Jones, 2023, p. 69).

When you travel to the airport or grocery store, signs guide you. You aren't required to use cognitive brain space for directions; easily accessible visuals provide this information instead. Similarly, classroom visuals can guide students in a way that reduces cognitive overload but still effectively communicates information. We explore this more deeply in the next section.

IMPLEMENTING EFFECTIVE COMMUNICATION

As the instructional leaders and facilitators of learning within classrooms, teachers need to be effective communicators. The student-engaged classroom depends on students' capability to work independently and navigate the learning environment. In order for them to do this successfully, you need to clearly communicate two main types of expectations to students throughout the day: (1) behavior expectations and (2) learning expectations.

CLEAR BEHAVIOR EXPECTATIONS

Think about how many interactions you have with students in a day and how you communicate expectations, procedures, and directions. Chances are, you are faced with student interruptions or find yourself repeating information. How often do you lose student engagement when giving instructions? Are your students receiving positive feedback because they are responsibly navigating their learning environment, or are they repeatedly hearing demands because they are not meeting expectations?

Visibly posting expectations saves you from using your voice to reinforce expectations when it should be used for teaching. Effective visuals are thorough, are accessible to all students, and include pictures or symbols as needed based on students' age and developmental ability. The purpose of visuals is to communicate procedures nonverbally so students can continuously refer to them until those procedures become routine. The key to visual representations is student ownership. Instead of the teacher placing a directive or demand on a student, the student takes ownership by referring to the visual to guide their behavior. This autonomy develops students' independence and self-efficacy. According to Hattie (2023):

> Self-efficacy has one of the largest effects on learning of all will attributes. Self-efficacy is having the confidence that one will triumph, one can do the task, one knows how to ask for help, or one knows what to do when one does not know what to do. . . . It leads to a willingness to exert effort and persist toward a goal, and is about whether a student believes they can accomplish the task. (p. 94)

Begin by thinking of an area or time in your day when you constantly remind students to complete tasks or follow established procedures. It is helpful to chunk this reflection into specific times of your day, like arrival, dismissal, soft start (see page 45), lineup, movement to the carpet for whole-group instruction, small-group learning stations, and any other structures you have in your classroom. List those times of day and tasks in figure 1.1 (page 20). Reflect on how you currently provide explanations to students, and then brainstorm how you could create a visual to convey those expectations instead. Record your ideas in the last column. We provide examples in the chart.

Time of Day	Task, Practice, or Procedure	Visual Needed
Morning start	Greeting the teacher	A welcome sign that reads, "Choose a way to greet the teacher," with optional greetings (hug, fist bump, or high five) hung on the door
Morning circle	Coming to the carpet	A picture of the class sitting in a circle and facing one another, with everyone in their own space, projected for students to refer to
Recess, specials, and dismissal	Transitioning out of the room and lining up	A picture of the class lining up in order, standing quietly and ready to leave the room
Transitions	Walking in the hallway	A picture of a student or character holding a finger up to their mouth to remind students to remain quiet in the hallway

FIGURE 1.1: Application activity—Visuals to communicate expectations.

*Visit **go.SolutionTree.com/instruction** for a free reproducible version of this figure.*

To create each visual, write down all the procedural steps it takes for students to complete the task. Create a poster or other visual with each step and a picture representing the expectation. Hang this in the room where students can see it. Visuals can include pictures of appropriate behavior, like a student sitting on a dot spot on the carpet or within a carpet square. Pictures can represent clean cubbies or desks. These visuals are more impactful when your current students are in them, demonstrating the appropriate way to do things. When students ask questions about a routine, the teacher can communicate expectations by pointing to the picture, instead of placing a verbal demand on the students, to reiterate what is expected. Or the teacher can display the picture in that learning area as a model for students to follow. The picture can also be held up or pointed to as a silent reminder for students not following directions.

An easy way to develop and display procedures is to create and project a slideshow using Google Slides, Canva, or PowerPoint. Figure 1.2 provides an example of a visual teachers can create and use in their classrooms to help students follow an established procedure for cleaning up. It gives simple and clear directions that kindergarten and first-grade students can follow quickly and easily, and includes a digital countdown timer that ensures students know how much time they have left to complete the procedure.

Communication, Accountability, and Relationships   21

FIGURE 1.2: Example visual to help students follow a cleanup procedure.

The good-morning slide in figure 1.3 provides information pertaining to the day's date, which specials students have for the day, and steps students need to complete right away. Similar to figure 1.2, it includes a digital timer to help students manage their time when they arrive to class.

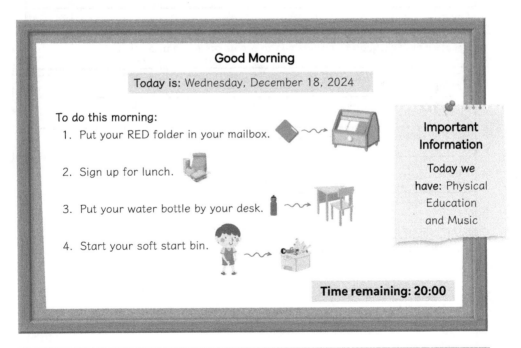

FIGURE 1.3: Example visual to help students follow a morning start-up procedure.

Finally, the small-group rotation breakdown in figure 1.4 also includes a timer; a visual of the Check, Check, Done! checklist students are expected to use during the rotation; and clear written directions for students to refer back to when they work independently. (Note all underlined items in this figure represent links students can interact with.)

Small Groups

Pick an activity from each section on your Check, Check, Done! to complete.

Move your NAME on the PROGRESSION BOARD when you complete an activity!

Check, Check, Done!

Foundations for Classroom Transformation

Collaboration Station	
Recreate a robot you read about with snap bricks. Write a paragraph explaining your robot.	
Create a Google Slide about the robot you read about on Newsela.	
Create a <u>five things poster</u> about a specific robot.	
Create a multiplication coloring sheet to create an image of a robot.	
Minilesson Station	
Identify text and graphic features from an article about robots (RI.3.5).	
Ask and answer questions from the article on robots (RI.3.1).	
Create a story, including dialogue, with at least one character being a robot; include facts you have learned about robots.	
List the sequence of events from the story you read about robots.	
Independent Work Station	
Write a narrative about your robot friend. Include dialogue! Don't forget to indent.	
Complete a character analysis for your robot.	
Complete the stoplight activity.	
Revise and edit your narrative.	
Type and print your narrative.	
Upload your narrative to Seesaw.	

Digital Content Station
Read and watch videos on Epic! about robots.
Read Newsela articles on robots.
Watch the Zume pizza robot video.
Watch the dialogue-writing video.
Watch the sequence-of-events video.
Watch the gorilla robot video.

Time remaining: 10:00 — Rotation 1

Source for standard: National Governors Association (NGA) Center for Best Practices & Council of Chief State School Officers (CCSSO), 2010a.

FIGURE 1.4: Example visual to help students follow small-group procedures.

Visuals like the examples in this section provide clear directions and are accessible for students to refer to independently instead of always relying on the teacher for guidance. To begin, create a visual checklist for students to refer to as they start their day. This is made simple for lower-elementary students (grades K–2) by using the labels *first* and *then* to organize the order in which the students should accomplish their tasks. For students in upper-elementary grades (grades 3–5), sequentially numbering the list helps students efficiently move through their tasks in order. If students are stuck or working unproductively, simply point to the progression board to get them back on track, or use your fingers to show step 1, step 2, and so on. These nonverbal signals do not take much time to redirect students, and they save teachers from having to repeat directions multiple times.

You can also post daily schedules in the room with times and pictures for students to refer to so they know what learning is taking place and what is coming next. Daily schedules help alleviate questions about what is to come and prevent the need for you to repeat procedures and expectations. Students can answer these questions themselves when they refer to the visual signposts that are in place around the room. Individual schedules can be printed, laminated, and placed on student desks, and students can cross off events as they happen throughout the day. Figure 1.5 (page 24) shows an example of a visual placed on students' desks. Make copies of this visual, and put them on your students' desks. Add pictures and times as desired.

Soft Start	Recess
Writing	Lunch
Specials	Mathematics
Literacy	Social Studies and Science
Small Groups	Dismissal

FIGURE 1.5: Example visual of the daily schedule on students' desks.

When implementing visuals that align with your procedures, starting small is best. Take the time up front to create a visual that helps students follow directions for one daily routine. Practice this routine with the visual and verbal cues multiple times, and then post the visual in the classroom. Continue to nonverbally refer to the visual until you notice most students efficiently completing the routine.

Students need lots of repetition to learn a new skill. According to James Clear (n.d.), "On average, it takes more than 2 months before a new behavior becomes automatic—66 days to be exact." Repeat this process with other procedures throughout the day; students will require consistent practice for at least two months before a routine is automatic. As the year goes on, if you find yourself constantly repeating a direction, if transitions are taking too long, or if instructional time is being wasted on logistic things, that is a sign your students may need more tools or systems to function on their own. Look for ways to replace verbal demands with visuals or tools that shift responsibility to students to sustain effective, clear communication.

CLEAR LEARNING EXPECTATIONS

Understanding your grade-level standards and understanding your current curriculum are the first steps to implementing and communicating clear learning expectations. Read the standards you are expected to teach, and prioritize the grade-specific goals students must reach by the end of the year. According to Thomas W. Many (former superintendent, author, and educational consultant) and Ted Horrell (superintendent; 2022):

> The goal is to create clear, consistent, and coherent commitments among the faculty around what all students must know and be able to do. This is accomplished by examining the standards, one at a time, through the lens of the R.E.A.L. criteria. (p. 3)

R.E.A.L. stands for *readiness, endurance, assessed,* and *leverage.* When teachers look at standards collectively in an effort to prioritize them, they need to determine whether the standard prepares students so they are ready for the next grade or course, whether the standard has knowledge and skills that endure beyond the current grade level and stand the test of time, whether the standard is assessed on high-stakes assessments, and whether the standard leverages knowledge and skills that occur in other content areas and have cross-curricular connections.

Once standards are prioritized, grade-level teams can begin the process of unwrapping them together. Authors Larry Ainsworth and Kyra Donovan (2019) describe *unwrapping* as "analyzing and deconstructing the wording of grade-level and course-specific priority standards within each unit of study to determine exactly what students need to know (teachable concepts) and be able to do (specific skills)" (p. 99). This process can be completed by identifying the nouns (what students need to know) and verbs (what skills students need to do) within each standard. As an example, table 1.1 shows two different unwrapped standards for English language arts.

TABLE 1.1: Examples of Unwrapped Standards

RI.1.1: Ask and answer questions about key details in a text.	
Concepts (Nouns)	**Skills (Verbs)**
Questions Key details	Ask Answer
RL.4.2: Determine a theme of a story, drama, or poem from details in the text; summarize the text.	
Concepts (Nouns)	**Skills (Verbs)**
Theme of a story, drama, or poem Details Text	Determine Summarize

Source for standards: NGA & CCSSO, 2010a.

It is important for teachers to define and explain the concepts that are embedded in the standards to ensure students are clear about what is expected of them. For the first example standard in table 1.1 (page 25), defining *key details* will help first graders fully understand what they are asking and answering questions about. From the unwrapped standard, teachers can create learning targets in student-friendly language that help make the standard approachable and clear to students— for example, "I can ask questions about what I read" and "I can answer questions about details in the text."

In the second example in table 1.1, fourth graders will need to be able to understand what a theme is and how a story, a drama, and a poem are different. For further clarity, teachers will also need to define what it means to determine a theme. Learning targets for this standard could be, "I can determine the theme of a story by using details" and "I can summarize a poem." Create a focus wall in your classroom to display these learning targets. Introduce the learning goals when you begin a study unit, and provide examples of proficient work that meet the standard for students to reference as a guide when they are working. Revisit the learning targets throughout the unit, ensuring they are visible and relevant to student learning.

Finally, it's important to communicate learning expectations to families as well. As the Common Core State Standards Initiative (n.d.) suggests, "With students, parents, and teachers all on the same page and working together toward shared goals, we can ensure that students make progress each year and graduate from high school prepared to succeed in college, career, and life." In this way, presenting learning expectations accessibly and in student-friendly language, with examples of proficient work, makes the expectations much clearer and more attainable for students.

The Role of Accountability

In the elementary classroom, it's expected that students will get off task, wander the room, or engage in behaviors disruptive to instruction or peer learning, often leaving the teacher and other students feeling disrespected. For this reason, the student-engaged framework relies heavily on students taking responsibility for their learning, remaining engaged, completing tasks, and meeting their learning goals. After you clearly communicate classroom expectations to students, you need to hold them accountable (responsible) for their behavior and academic learning. Without accountability, chaos ensues in the learning environment as learning remains stagnant, as if everyone's wheels are just spinning. To ensure accountability, students need structure and guidance, and they are capable of self-managing and holding each other accountable. Education writer and superintendent Derrick Meador (2019) emphasizes:

> In a structured learning environment, students are more likely to thrive and experience personal and academic growth. Too often teachers provide students with freedoms that they can abuse. A lack of structure can destroy a learning environment and undermine a teacher's authority, leading to misbehavior and wasted time.

Writing for the School Planner Company, Brad Holmes (2024) further explains that teaching self-accountability to students is a challenging task, but that "once students feel a sense of ownership and control over their academic success, they will be more invested in the learning process." This sense of ownership and control will help students develop time management and organizational skills.

Let's look closer at the impact on students who feel held accountable for their learning and some high-impact strategies you can implement in your classroom.

UNDERSTANDING ACCOUNTABILITY

Accountability is important in classrooms because it helps students develop the skills and habits they need to succeed in school and life. Feeling accountable at school means feeling invested in one's learning and improvement. According to Anjail Kenyatta (2020), director of content and curriculum development at the Center for Responsive Schools:

> When students hold themselves accountable for their progress, they not only excel academically but they also become more empowered and invested in their learning. Students are more likely to see failure as an opportunity to learn and are better able to accomplish the goals they set for themselves. (p. 16)

A student who is accountable for their learning is more likely to come to class prepared and work hard to accomplish tasks assigned to them. Students who are responsible for their own behavior are more apt to be respectful to their classmates and teachers and will follow classroom expectations. Accountable students also set challenging goals for themselves and work hard to achieve them. As detailed in this book's introduction (page 1), John Hattie's (2015) meta-analyses identify the effect sizes of various influences within education and find the average effect size to be 0.40. Any influence with an effective size greater than this hinge point is considered effective in the classroom, particularly influences with effect sizes that approach 0.80 or higher. Hattie (2015) identifies the following effect sizes for each of these factors that relate to accountability in the classroom.

- Self-efficacy: 0.92
- Work completion and effort: 0.77
- Self-reflection of learning targets: 0.75
- Teacher feedback: 0.70
- Goal setting: 0.68

These factors hold students accountable and result in high student achievement, and we explore various strategies for implementing them into your classroom instruction in the next section.

IMPLEMENTING ACCOUNTABLE PRACTICES

The student-engaged framework runs effectively when students can work together and collaborate. They need to know how to get along, communicate, and rely on one another when they are working at stations and not receiving direct instruction from you. There are also times when students must be able to work independently. Therefore, the framework builds students' independence and interdependence because they are held accountable for their own work and how well they work with others. Teachers have several ways to nurture student accountability within the student-engaged framework, including goal setting; Brain, Buddy, Buddy (a form of peer check-in); time management; and team leaders.

STUDENT GOAL SETTING

To begin teaching goal setting and help students become familiar with the process of setting a goal, start with a fun goal the class can work on and track together. Do this by helping students choose an activity they would like to get better at while at school. Ideas for this might include things like the following.

- Drawing
- Tying their shoelaces
- Speaking a different language
- Doing origami
- Making a paper airplane
- Shooting a basket
- Snapping

Figure 1.6 lays out the process for setting a fun goal with students and tracking progress.

> **Our Class Goal:**
>
> We will go from 0% to 100% confidence in drawing by October 1.
>
> To meet our goal, we will follow these **action steps**!
> 1. Watch a drawing video four times a week on Art Hub.
> 2. Look at pictures of our animal four times a week.
>
> If we follow **both** action steps for that day, we will color the day green on our tracking sheet!
>
> If we follow **one** action step, we will color the day yellow.
>
> If we do not follow either action step, we will color the day red.

FIGURE 1.6: Fun goal example.

Once students have some experience with setting a goal and working toward it daily, you can increasingly and effectively align their goals to academics. And when clear learning targets are established and communicated with students, as detailed earlier in this chapter, they can be used for goal setting and self-reflection. Robert J. Marzano, Debra J. Pickering, and Jane E. Pollock (2001) believe "students should be encouraged to adapt [goals] to their personal needs and desires" (p. 95), and teachers should implement consistent feedback to help guide students' progress toward their goals. Feedback should "provide students with an explanation of what they are doing that is correct and what they are doing that is not correct" (Marzano et al., 2001, p. 96). Corrective feedback paired with proficiency scales, rubrics, and student work examples helps students clearly envision what is expected with learning targets. Over time, students can start monitoring and self-evaluating their own progress.

According to Anjail Kenyatta and Ellie Cornecelli (2020), student goals should be student centered and specific. We typically write SMART goals, with *SMART* standing for *strategic and specific, measurable, attainable, results oriented,* and *time bound* (Conzemius & O'Neill, 2014). When we set goals with students, we want them to be as specific as possible, focusing on one skill at a time; for example, a student would like to increase their fluency rate from the beginning of the school year to the end of the school year. To see progress, the goal must be measurable so we can track growth. If the student begins the year reading twenty-five correct words per minute and wants to increase this to sixty-six correct words per minute to make their benchmark in May, they will need to increase by forty-one words throughout the year. If we divide this by the number of weeks of instruction we have, it will average out to slightly over a word a week for growth.

This is an attainable goal for the student, but it takes intentional action steps to achieve it. The student needs to determine two action steps they want to accomplish every day that will lead them toward their goal. Although there are multiple paths to accomplish this goal, the student will need support in deciding which two action steps are doable within instructional time. For example, maybe they will practice decoding CVC words to build accuracy. Once a week, they will read a list of CVC words to an adult with 100 percent accuracy. This adult could be a reading support teacher, a paraprofessional, or the office secretary. We find that we can be creative in supporting our students' action steps by having all hands on deck within our building. If adults are limited, the student could record their reading of these words and the teacher could help monitor progress biweekly. Another action this student could take would be to practice reading a short passage multiple times and timing their reading for a minute to track their progress from week to week. The key to action steps is doing them consistently, within a determined time frame, and action steps must be realistic so students can complete them.

As teachers, we can check growth at benchmark intervals to monitor if what students are doing is working (results oriented). After a specified number of weeks (time bound; this can be flexible depending on the urgency of the goal), the student will read a passage for one minute with the teacher and measure if they have grown three to four words in their fluency rate. Depending on the data collected within the action steps and the benchmark data, the student may need to adjust their action steps if they are not working and the student is not progressing. These decisions should be made with the help of the teacher. Having intervals of working through action steps and checking benchmark data throughout the year keeps the goal timely and at the forefront of both students' and teachers' minds.

It is important to note in this example that several factors affect the fluency goal the student has set, and changes to the student's independent practice are a small piece of the bigger picture. Adjustments to the goal's action steps may not be necessary, and the student may continue with their goal plan while the teacher adjusts their direct instruction to meet the student's needs. Scheduling time to check in with students on their goal work can help drive instruction when goals are relevant and aligned to standards.

The goal-setting sheet in figure 1.7 provides a way for students to track their effort toward their goal every week. First, they state their goal in measurable terms so it is constantly visible to them. In this example, the student tracks their effort toward the goal.

Goal:
Read sixty-six words per minute by May.

Was I able to complete **two** action steps related to my goal today?
Color your square.

- **Green** = Two action steps completed
- **Yellow** = One action step completed
- **Red** = Zero action steps completed

Monday	Tuesday	Wednesday	Thursday	Friday

Friday reflection:

How many green days? | 2 |

What I want to continue **or** do differently next week to work toward my goal:

Reread sentence

Practice memory words

FIGURE 1.7: Completed student goal-setting form.

Visit *go.SolutionTree.com/instruction* for a free reproducible version of this figure.

Setting goals for work completion can motivate students to complete tasks and is a simple way to begin the goal-setting process. Students will track the number of action steps they complete daily. They can determine action steps with the help of their teacher, or if you are trying to build independence and autonomy, have students ask themselves, "What are two things I can do today that will get me closer to my goal?" Students record two actions they can commit to daily to get better and work toward their goal. As students practice completing this goal tracker, help them see how their work completion impacts their academic achievement.

Every day, give students five to ten minutes to reflect and record their progress with an *accountability buddy*, a partner within the class who helps the student stay on track with their goal. Accountability buddies check in with one another and ask reflection questions to help guide and support self-reflection and growth. Teach students to ask each other, "What action steps did you take to work on your goal today?" If a student cannot name two things they worked on, their accountability buddy should ask, "What got in the way of working on your goal today?" After goal conversations occur, each student should color-code their progress toward their goal. If the student completed two action steps toward their goal, they may color their daily box green. If they completed only one action, they may color the box yellow, and if no action steps were completed, the daily box should be colored red.

At the end of the week, accountability buddies get together to reflect on their weekly progress. Buddies should discuss what could have hindered work on student goals. If some students have mostly red squares, indicating a failure to work toward their goal, accountability buddies should help them determine why. Together, they can brainstorm ways to support each other, such as checking in more often or practicing together. As students gain proficiency in this process, teach them to look for patterns in their successes and failures to reflect on their progress and whether they accomplished their action steps. For example, are there certain days of the week when they accomplish more tasks? Why or why not? Are certain tasks more difficult for them to complete than others? Helping each other reflect on their behavioral tendencies and learning from their mistakes are the purposes of these conversations.

Through this peer-to-peer feedback process around goal setting, students empower each other, but it's a process they will need you, as their teacher, to model for them. For example, you might ask a colleague to help you model conversational skills by role playing in front of students. Build these conversational skills by having students practice these conversations and hold each other accountable for their actions. Peer-to-peer reflection can be a powerful motivator for students. Once you've modeled this process for students, it's important that you give them a chance to figure out this process themselves with the help of a peer before intervening. Use figure 1.8 to model and help students guide themselves through one of these conversations.

Ask your partner the following questions, and record their answers.

☐ **What action steps did you take to work on your goal?**

Listen for them to state specific actions. Write down what they say.

1. _____
2. _____

If your partner doesn't have two action steps that they worked on, ask the following.

☐ **What got in the way of working on your action steps?**

Write down what they say.

_____
_____

> ☐ **What supports do you need next week to help you get more action steps done?**
> Write down what they say.
> _____
> _____
>
> ☐ **What can you do differently to accomplish more action steps next week?**
> Write down what they say.
> _____
> _____
>
> Switch roles and have your partner ask you these reflection questions.

FIGURE 1.8: Goal reflection conversation for accountability buddies.

Visit go.SolutionTree.com/instruction for a free reproducible version of this figure.

Learning this process will be messy and take time. These things come with building independence in your students and creating a student-centered classroom. However, if after a couple of weeks of trialing this process, you notice some students are still not working on their goal and have a lot of red boxes, check in with those students individually. They may need additional support from an adult.

BRAIN, BUDDY, BUDDY

Another strategy that places responsibility on students and holds them accountable for their learning is Brain, Buddy, Buddy. With the Brain, Buddy, Buddy strategy, students check in with themselves and then check in with two of their peers if they have a question. You can use this strategy with students who need support or have questions when working independently while you are working with other students. This strategy builds self-reliance by encouraging students to check in with themselves first before they seek help from others.

Students often have the answers they seek within their brains or have the skills to tap into resources to figure out their questions before they ask someone else. Of course, there are times when students will need assistance from others. This strategy places responsibility back onto students, instead of teaching them to always rely on others, and frees you from unnecessary interruptions during direct instruction.

Students who ask a lot of questions can impact how well other students learn because questions can disrupt the lesson flow, making it difficult for some students to focus. Could these questions be answered if students checked in with themselves and their peers before they came to the teacher? As a teacher, you may have told students, "Ask three before me," which teaches students to always check with other students before coming to you. In the student-engaged classroom, you will use the common language of the Brain, Buddy, Buddy strategy, which teaches students to first rely on themselves to see if they can figure out the answer before asking a peer. This strategy holds students accountable for checking in with themselves first and then with other students while helping each other navigate the learning environment.

To introduce Brain, Buddy, Buddy, assign buddies for students. Figure 1.9 is a desk label students can use to write down their buddies.

FIGURE 1.9: Desk label for students to write down and remember who their buddies are.

Visit **go.SolutionTree.com/instruction** *for a free reproducible version of this figure.*

Initially, when grouping students, you may need to do this randomly or let students select their partners because you won't know your students' strengths yet. If everyone is included and has a partner, letting students choose at the beginning of the year won't harm anyone. Once you get to know your students, systematically place students who need more support with more proficient role models who can help them communicate and model executive functioning skills throughout learning stations. There isn't a right or wrong amount of time that buddies are assigned to each other. However, start by having students paired up for two weeks, and adjust based on your observations of student interactions. Are students utilizing the Brain, Buddy, Buddy system? Are the numbers of unnecessary interruptions within small groups and during direct instruction decreasing from what you typically experience? If so, then the system is working. If some students habitually come to you first and have trouble implementing Brain, Buddy, Buddy, it will take consistency on your part to redirect students to their peers before they ask you. It is also imperative that, as a class, you define unnecessary interruptions and differentiate times when students are allowed to interrupt direct instruction. Situations where an adult is needed, such as someone being hurt, are always appropriate interruptions to instruction. A question about an assignment is not an appropriate interruption because a peer can answer it. Clarifying the difference will help strengthen the purpose of the Brain, Buddy, Buddy system by fostering interdependence among students.

When redirecting students, simply pointing to the visual on their worksheet or saying "Brain, Buddy, Buddy" is effective. Create a hat or crown labeled "Brain, Buddy, Buddy," and wear it when working with some students in a small group. Teach students not to interrupt you if you are wearing the hat. After students catch on to the system and utilize Brain, Buddy, Buddy consistently, let them decide who their buddies will be. Offering this choice provides more autonomy to independent workers who are completing their work.

TIME MANAGEMENT

Effective time management encourages accountability and plays a crucial role in work completion because it allows individuals to effectively allocate and utilize their time to accomplish tasks and goals. By setting specific timelines for completing tasks and monitoring progress against these timelines, students individually hold themselves accountable for their work completion.

Time management can be learned using visual timers; for example, you can embed a virtual timer in your slides to communicate how much time students have left to complete assignments and tasks. (Refer to figure 1.3, page 21.) The student-engaged framework thrives on students' ability to complete work independently by minimizing distractions and staying focused on the task at hand. This focused attention improves productivity and ensures that work is completed without unnecessary delays.

Time management also involves planning ahead, which allows individuals to anticipate potential obstacles and allocate resources accordingly. When switching from one subject to another, transitioning students with a one-minute timer (or less) can eliminate wasted time. To implement timers, time a current transition that is taking longer than expected. Communicate to students how long the transition takes, and set a class goal to gather materials more quickly and be ready for the next activity. Have students think about the materials they need ahead of time, continuing to track the amount of transition time, and see how much instructional time you save as a class when a timer is utilized. As students become efficient at transitions, pair them with quick movement activities, like yoga poses or gross motor actions, to engage students' bodies and brains as they transition for a minute amid learning.

TEAM LEADERS

During collaboration or group work, it is important to have a student facilitate and lead this work. Often, when students work together in groups, conflict can arise. Some students may remain off task and not contribute to the group. Others may complain or constantly disagree with group decisions, which in turn disrupts productivity. Team leaders can help the groups solve these situations and refocus everyone so work gets accomplished.

You can use team leaders at any grade level, though students' responsibilities and what they are reporting on may look different depending on their age. In kindergarten or first grade, team leaders may ensure everyone has the correct materials out and is ready to work. Third- and fourth-grade students could assign group members roles, such as timekeeper, recorder, and organizer, to collect all necessary materials. In these upper-elementary grades, team leaders would manage their peers within these roles to make sure everyone is contributing and being responsible within the group.

When students collaborate in groups of three or four to complete an activity or project during instructional times, team leaders can help manage this collaboration. Students apply or are recommended for the team lead position. Once the teacher selects the leader, they are then responsible for keeping the group on task and ensuring the group completes their project or task on time. This is an earned position; students may be removed if they do not fulfill the requirements. If students are productive team leaders and collaborative work is completed productively, team leads may stay in the position longer.

You will need to teach students how to be a team leader and what qualities a student must have to hold the role. According to Carlee Strathmann (n.d.), project manager for XQ Institute, an organization that advocates for helping young people gain leadership skills, good leaders' qualities begin with excellent communication. They are future focused on the vision or task at hand. They inspire and motivate others to join them in shared goals or a common learning destination. A good team leader is open-minded to others' ideas, receptive to feedback, and a team player. They want all to succeed and help others along the way. You can create a bank of questions or tasks that the team leader would need to enforce, such as the following.

- Does everyone have their supplies?
- Are all members aware of what they should be doing?
- Is everyone on task?
- Does anyone have any questions?

These questions can help team leaders effectively facilitate work time within their group. In a kindergarten classroom, the team leader could look for work completion, ready materials, and on-task students. They could report these things to the teacher in visuals such as emoji faces or colors like green, yellow, and red.

In addition to having a guide for the team leader, it is helpful to equip the other students with clear guidelines for their roles. One way to establish these is to create a rubric of expectations. Criteria in the rubric could include whether the group member is staying on task, collaborating with others, and displaying a strong work ethic and responsibility. At the end of the week, group members self-evaluate how they contributed to the group and met the criteria items. Using the rubric, group members also evaluate how each group member contributed and how the team leader performed. This system of checks and balances provides data for the teacher to see how effectively each group member completed tasks and worked with peers. Figure 1.10 shows an example of a rubric students can use to self-evaluate during group work.

Criteria	Proficient (3)	Developing (2)	Below Expectations (1)
On-task and focused behavior	Consistently focused on achieving group goals Does not distract group members	Occasionally focused on achieving group goals Occasionally distracts group members (one or two times, but gets back on track when redirected)	Rarely or never focused on achieving group goals Distracts group members and derails group work
Collaboration with others	Actively listens to others Supports others' ideas	Occasionally listens to and supports others	Rarely listens to and supports others Ignores others' ideas
Communication skills	Clearly shares ideas and actively contributes to group work Takes turns talking and sharing	Occasionally communicates effectively	Rarely communicates effectively Interrupts others
Responsibility and reliability	Always completes assigned tasks on time	Occasionally completes assigned tasks on time	Rarely completes assigned tasks on time
Conflict resolution	Effectively resolves conflict within the group	Occasionally helps resolve conflict within the group	Rarely or never helps resolve conflict within the group

FIGURE 1.10: Collaboration rubric example.

*Visit **go.SolutionTree.com/instruction** for a free reproducible version of this figure.*

The Role of Relationships

When it comes to student success in the classroom, relationships are key. The student-engaged framework focuses on strong student-to-teacher relationships (built through trust) and student-to-student relationships (built through completion of collaborative work at the learning stations). When the framework is implemented and running in a classroom, teachers need to be able to trust that students are completing work, working collaboratively, and self-managing while they (teachers) are immersed in small-group direct instruction. That trust comes from knowing your students and building a strong community of interdependent learners. Trust is reciprocal in a classroom; for students to invest in the learning, they need to feel that their teacher knows and understands them, designs learning opportunities to meet their academic needs, and incorporates their interests. As Robert Marzano (2016) says:

> When teachers reach out to students to attempt to understand their backgrounds and interests, it shows students that the teacher is interested in their lives as individuals, not just students, and helps them feel more accepted in the classroom and more trusting of the teacher. (p. 2)

As humans, we need connection. International speaker and lecturer at the Yale School of Management Emma Seppälä (2014) states:

> People who feel more connected to others have lower levels of anxiety and depression. Moreover, studies show they also have higher self-esteem, greater empathy for others, are more trusting and cooperative and, as a consequence, others are more open to trusting and cooperating with them. In other words, social connectedness generates a positive feedback loop of social, emotional and physical well-being.

Seppälä (2014) further states that connection to peers establishes trust, leading to cooperation. When students can connect, they can collaborate, work together, and develop interpersonal skills in classrooms that will eventually transfer to the workforce.

Let's look closer at the impact on learning when students have healthy relationships with their teacher and peers.

UNDERSTANDING SCHOOL RELATIONSHIPS

Relationships create a sense of belonging and safety. When students feel like they are part of a community and safe and supported, they are more likely to be engaged in their learning. Or as author, consultant, and former special education teacher Trynia Kaufman (n.d.) puts it, "Positive student relationships are fundamental to success. When students feel supported, they're more likely to engage in learning and have better academic outcomes." Students with positive relationships with their teachers and peers are also more likely to be motivated to learn and participate in class activities (Wang, 2023).

When strong relationships are established, students can turn to their teachers and peers for help with academics, social problems, or other challenges. Positive social behavior can be modeled through interactions when adults and peers serve as role models and show how to interact with others respectfully and productively. According to the University of Cambridge (2016), "Researchers found that students with a more positive relationship with their teacher displayed towards peers, on average, 18% more prosocial behaviour, and up to 38% less aggressive behaviour, over students who felt ambivalent or negative toward their teacher."

Overall, positive relationships at school can help students develop a positive self-image and build resilience. Students who have strong relationships with teachers and peers are more likely to achieve high grades, attend school regularly, graduate from high school, go on to college, and earn more money later in life. According to the National Center on Safe Supportive Learning Environments (2023):

> Students who feel connected to school are more likely to succeed—they have better school attendance, grades, and test scores and stay in school longer. Students who attend classrooms with higher emotional support are more likely to exert effort to understand difficult concepts.

Students with positive relationships are more likely to develop strong social skills like communication, cooperation, and conflict resolution. By fostering positive relationships, schools can create a more supportive and productive learning environment for all students.

IMPLEMENTING PRACTICES FOR POSITIVE RELATIONSHIPS

Several strategies exist to build strong relationships among teachers and students, and you can begin building these relationships on day one. Smile and greet your students at the door every morning when they come in. Before school starts, host a meet-and-greet, where students can come into the classroom to drop off supplies and get comfortable in their learning space. This is a great opportunity to meet parents and welcome them into the classroom community.

Another effective way to begin the school year on a positive note is to reach out to and connect with parents. Each school day, during the first month of school, take ten to fifteen minutes after school to call three parents. Share something positive you notice about their student. Taking the time to do this up front proactively shows parents you are optimistic and see the good within their child. We have observed that if parents feel you seek the positive and potential in your students, they will be more willing to listen when you address growth areas because they will know it comes from a place of caring.

The first contact with parents should never result from their child misbehaving; beginning the year with negative interactions is counterproductive to the relationships you are trying to build. Positive phone calls fill parents' emotional buckets and will foster more future collaboration opportunities. Investing in this time will pay off throughout the year because parents will trust you are doing what is best for their child. Positive interactions will continue to happen, and open communication will help parents and teachers work together to help students be successful. Bridging connections between school and home sends students the message that where they come from is valued and we are all working together to benefit their growth as humans and learners.

In addition to these initial relationship-building strategies, you can further cement your positive relationships with students through strategies like class meetings, learner portfolios, conversation partners, soft start, and academic conversations.

CLASS MEETINGS

Schedule daily classroom meetings for the first couple of weeks of school so students can share about themselves, providing every student with a voice. These meetings can take place in a short amount of time; just ten to fifteen minutes is typically enough time to have everyone share. Begin by asking questions, and have students ask questions to help get students to open up. As the year goes on, schedule morning meetings to check in. Have students sit in one big circle so everyone is facing each other, and give everyone a chance to have a voice and share.

During this time, have students practice active listening skills, and ensure that no one gets interrupted when they put their voice into the room. Share stories about yourself and be vulnerable with your students. Admit when you make mistakes and own them in front of your students to model that mistakes are part of growing. Sharing your human side with students helps them connect with, relate to, and learn from you.

Protect this time throughout the year, and use it to continue to get to know the people in your classroom community. If a conflict arises, this time can also be utilized to problem-solve and empower students to help formulate solutions. As the year progresses, gradually release the responsibility of facilitating the meeting to students so they can lead.

LEARNER PORTFOLIOS

One tool you can use to build relationships is the learner portfolio, which is a collection of evidence that documents and demonstrates an individual's learning journey over time. These portfolios are often used to showcase learners' achievements, progress, and reflections across various subjects or skills. You can implement learner portfolios at the start of the school year to get to know your students better. Marzano (2016) says, "Understanding students' backgrounds and interests can create an atmosphere of cooperation in a classroom and decrease classroom disruptions" (p. 5).

Setting up an initial digital learning profile as the first entry in a student portfolio makes easy the implementation of a portfolio that will expand throughout the year. You can create a slideshow with questions and prompts and have students fill them out. Figure 1.11 is an example of a learning profile that students fill out at the beginning of the school year and can revisit throughout the year.

My Learning Profile
Cody Castillo

My Likes and Dislikes

Likes
- I like pizza.
- I like taking pictures.
- I like shopping.
- I like reading.
- I like listening to music.

Dislikes
- I don't like feeling stressed.
- I don't like waking up early.
- I don't like mean people.
- I don't like when people don't listen to me.
- I don't like pork.

FIGURE 1.11: Student learner profile example. continued ▶

Visit go.SolutionTree.com/instruction for a free reproducible version of this figure.

> **My Learning Preferences**
>
> I learn best when our classroom . . .
> - (has soft music) / is quiet
>
> I work best . . .
> - by myself / (with a partner) / in a group
>
> I learn best by . . .
> - hearing or listening / (seeing words or pictures) / doing a hands-on activity
>
> The way I learn best in our classroom is . . .
> - sitting on the floor / being at a standing desk / (sitting on a wobble stool) / being in a table group / sitting at my desk, moved away from people / sitting at the low desk / standing at my desk / (lying on the floor)
>
> I learn best in the . . .
> - (morning) / afternoon
>
> I get excited about learning when . . .
>
> <u>I get to create things</u>

These examples provide insights and can begin with questions that help you learn more about each student's interests and feelings toward learning, such as the following.

- What do you do for fun?
- What are your strengths?
- How do you prefer to share your learning with others?
- What interests do you have or what is important to you?

Although these questions are tailored more for upper-elementary students, you could adapt them for students in grades K–2 by adding more visual prompts or using a "this or that" format. Students' social-emotional learning and self-image can also be gauged by asking questions such as the following.

- What makes you upset?
- What helps you when you are upset?
- What are you proud of?
- What are some words you would want people to use to describe you?

As the year progresses, learner portfolios can communicate a lot about student learning. You can incorporate goal setting into learner portfolios by collecting evidence and creating reflection slides for students to track their progress on specific standards. Students can upload work examples, or you can ask students specific questions on slides for them to complete as formative assessments that align to learning standards. This would be a way to systematically collect work in one place for all expected standards you ask students to be proficient in. Setting this up at the beginning of the year would take time. However, students could compile work throughout the whole school year. You can add reflection questions to the bottom of each slide for students to self-assess according to proficiency scales.

Writing portfolios are another great way to get to know your students through their ideas, opinions, and thoughts. You can use several writing prompts to connect with your students, and these can easily be added to slides in their digital portfolios.

Whether you want to get to know your students personally or academically, learner portfolios are a critical tool to help you build strong relationships. Start small by determining your purpose. What do you want to know about when it comes to your students? Although slides are efficient because they are editable, can be adjusted throughout the year, and are all in one place, you can create a worksheet with questions that help you better understand what your students like and what motivates and frustrates them. These can be collected and kept in student files to refer to. Continue asking students throughout the year to see if interests change, to gauge students' feelings toward their learning, and to consistently give them a voice. Everyone wants to be checked in with and heard; students are no different.

CONVERSATION PARTNERS

Students need an opportunity to talk, get to know each other, and build relationships. Conversation partners build peer relationships. Start by allotting three to five minutes daily when students can partner up and have a one-on-one conversation. The conversation format needs to be taught and modeled so students are asking each other questions, actively listening, and responding positively. Students need to learn how to take turns talking and share back-and-forth exchanges so the conversation is authentic and two-sided.

With a colleague or coach, model how to have a social conversation. Use the conversation partner anchor chart in figure 1.12 (page 44) as an example for your students. Take turns talking, asking each other questions, pausing to hear the response, and following up with another question or comment. Model appropriate body language. Show students how you are facing each other and making eye contact. Begin by assigning students to partners they will keep for the week. Ideally, you should partner a student who is more socially adept with a student who needs support with their communication skills so they can learn from their peers.

Start a Conversation

Ask Them a Question

- ☑ What did you do last night?
- ☑ What do you like to do after school?
- ☑ What do you like to watch on TV?
- ☑ What are you doing this weekend?

Continue a Conversation

Listen and Think

Your partner responds to the comment or question.

> Listen to their response
> AND
> think about what they are saying.

Make a Positive Comment
OR Ask a Question

> Make a positive comment
> OR
> ask a question about the topic.

Listen and Think

Your partner responds to the comment or question.

> Listen to their response
> AND
> think about what they are saying.

Make a Positive Comment
OR Ask a Question

> Make a positive comment
> OR
> ask a question about the topic.

Thank your partner for sharing, and then switch roles!

FIGURE 1.12: Conversation partner anchor chart.

*Visit **go.SolutionTree.com/instruction** for a free reproducible version of this figure.*

Figure 1.13 shows creative ways to partner students up. For example, assign students peanut butter and jelly partners, or use chips and salsa partners. When students need to partner up, direct them to find their peanut butter–jelly partner or chips–salsa partner. At the beginning of the year, you may not know much about your students, making it difficult to pair students up systematically. As conversation partners continue, you will quickly learn who can carry on a conversation and who needs more support.

Person 1	Person 2
Person with strong communication skills	Person with a lack of communication skills (The students named in this column will be the ones you rotate throughout the weeks to pair them up with strong communicators.)
Chips	Salsa
Mac	Cheese
Cookies	Milk
Peanut Butter	Jelly
Spaghetti	Meatballs

FIGURE 1.13: Partner chart ideas.

It is often difficult for students to initiate a conversation, so prompts are helpful to get the conversation going. Topics can range from what students did over the weekend to their favorite movie, book, or game. Aligning conversation topics to weekly social-emotional lessons strengthens the message. Anything goes if students can take turns, share with each other, and practice having authentic conversations. As conversation partners become systematic, rotate students through partners so students have a chance to build relationships with everyone in the class. If certain students have difficulty getting along or working together, intentionally pair them up so they can work through their issues together with support.

SOFT START

Another way to support student relationships is by implementing a soft start into the daily schedule. Instead of having students immediately get started on seatwork when they enter the classroom, a soft start provides a flexible transition into the school day. On entering the classroom, students unpack, sign up for lunch, sharpen pencils, and complete other morning tasks necessary to set them up for learning. Once students are prepared for the day, they go to their soft start bins with an assigned partner. Soft start bins offer a variety of typically nonacademic activities for students to complete; these can include Play-Doh™, building blocks, puzzles, or any activities that involve creativity, fine motor skills, and opportunities to interact and collaborate with a peer. This structured, scheduled part of the day allows students the flexibility of time when entering school. Students who arrive late don't miss direct instruction, and teachers and students can check in and talk with each other, further building positive relationships.

The first step after scheduling soft start is planning soft start activity bins and collecting materials. Labeling plastic storage bins with numbers helps organize materials. Assigning student partners in a pocket chart offers a visual for students to refer to, and having specific spaces in the room assigned for bins and activities keeps a soft start running efficiently. All components of soft start—partners, bins, and workspaces—may be labeled with coordinating numbers so students can navigate the room during the soft start time. For example, when first grader Lucas enters his classroom, he sees his name next to that of his partner, Ellie, in a pocket chart. They are pair number 7, meaning they are assigned to bin 7, magnetic tiles. A number 7 sign hangs above the back table, identifying the space where Lucas and Ellie need to head with their bin to build with the magnetic tiles.

Practicing these procedures and creating a visual slide with directions that include the soft start routine help guide students through this process. Including a timer and providing a couple of minutes for students to clean up keep the soft start to a concise time frame so students can still start their academic learning within a decent amount of time. It is also important that you provide directions for each soft start activity that students can refer to when they get out materials. The more systems you have in place for students to independently utilize, the more efficiently groups will run. Figure 1.14 features a checklist to walk you through implementing soft start bins. While the version shown here omits visual elements, consider using pictures of your classroom posters (such as good-morning procedures) and physical assets (such as soft start bins) to aid students' understanding.

Planning:
☐ Schedule a time for soft start bins (great to use when students arrive in the morning).

Visuals:
☐ Create a slide (such as a Google Slide or PowerPoint) with visuals to show students.
☐ Add time (duration) to the slide to help students manage their time.
☐ Include a transition slide with a timer and music for cleanup.

System:
☐ Assign partners for soft start bins. (You could use conversation partners or create new ones.)
☐ Label bins with numbers.
☐ Create a visual chart that has partners and bin numbers listed.

FIGURE 1.14: Soft start implementation checklist.

Next, let's consider some examples of soft start activities and explicit directions you might give to students. For each of the following, implement a slide or poster with the directions, and include a visual element to represent the activity. For example, if the activity includes the use of tangrams, you might include a picture of a tangram alongside the directions. As you review the following examples, consider how you might implement them in your classroom or what adjustments you might make for your students' unique needs.

- Tangrams
    a. Take your bin to a hard surface (table or desk) in the room.
    b. Select a picture to create with tangrams.
    c. Build your picture and discuss why you picked that picture.
    d. Share your picture with your partner.

- Building blocks (such as LEGO®)
    a. Take your blocks bin to an area on the floor.
    b. Pick a structure or something else to build with your partner. Is it going to be a museum? A business? A home?
    c. Talk with your partner while you're building about what you think goes into the building and creating of that structure.

- Play-Doh
    a. Take your bin to a hard surface (table or desk) in the room.
    b. Use the Play-Doh to create something you did over the summer.
    c. Take turns sharing what you created with your partner.
    d. Make sure you both get a chance to share.

- Coloring
    a. Take your bin to a hard surface (table or desk) in the room.
    b. Choose one coloring sheet to complete.
    c. Talk about how you are feeling today and why while you and your partner color.
    d. Make sure you both get a chance to share.

ACADEMIC CONVERSATIONS

Once relationships are built, students feel safe with each other, and trust has been built within the classroom, we can start to extend students' conversations into academic content. Elaborating on their own ideas and the ideas of others and justifying their thinking are major communication skills for students to learn. To do this, students will rely on the preceding foundational pieces and the relationships they have built. However, they need support articulating and expanding their thinking within conversation because this doesn't typically come naturally.

Elaborating on ideas involves expanding one's thoughts to provide more detail, context, and depth. This is something your students need you to teach them, and there are several different ways you can do this. To start, teach students that when they elaborate on ideas, they can provide examples that illustrate their points. Adding detail and explaining the who, what, where, when, why, and how aspects of an idea is another way to elaborate and explain in greater depth. When justifying ideas for someone else, they must back up the ideas with evidence, facts, or research findings because this lends credibility to the ideas as well.

To elaborate on and add to others' ideas, students also need to be good listeners and pay attention to details so they can expand and contribute to the academic conversation. Teaching students to listen closely as their peer is talking, to pull out key concepts, and to respond with a comment that connects and relates will extend thinking within the conversation.

Another strategy that gives students the opportunity to discuss academic content is accountable talk. According to Fisher and colleagues (2016), "Accountable talk is frequently framed as a set of expectations for students that is supported through the use of language frames that scaffold the use of language to explore a topic" (p. 144). Accountable talk provides talk moves and examples of questions students can ask one another to dive deeper into academic conversations and elaborate on their ideas. Conversation stems and prompts can help model and scaffold how to begin these discussions. Giving students time to dive deep into content and learn from one another through academic conversation is essential in developing critical thinkers within our classrooms.

Conclusion

Providing clear communication about behavior and learning expectations, holding students accountable to build self-efficacy, and fostering positive relationships within your classroom build skills that support the implementation of the student-engaged framework. When these skills are present in students, they are able to navigate learning stations independently, collaborate interdependently, and take full ownership of their education.

In the next chapter, we will discuss personalized learning tools that, when paired with the communication, accountability, and relationship skills we described in this chapter, build a strong foundation for the successful implementation of the student-engaged framework.

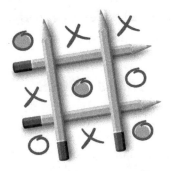

CHAPTER 2
PERSONALIZED LEARNING TOOLS

Mrs. Hubler's fourth-grade classroom is a vibrant learning hub where students are empowered to take ownership of their learning journey. Self-management tools are woven into her classroom, fostering independence, motivation, and a sense of ownership.

Visuals adorn the walls, guiding students through their daily tasks and routines. Each student has their own checklist, with multiple modes of instructional activities to meet all learning preferences. As they complete each task, they proudly check it off, walk up to the progression board, and move their game piece to the next level—all while enjoying a sense of accomplishment and progress.

Flexible seating allows students to choose the learning environment that best suits their needs. Some prefer the comfort of standing tables, while others thrive at individual desks. Some students opt for the quiet corner, while others prefer the collaborative buzz of group tables. The flexibility empowers students to create a learning space that fosters their focus and productivity.

Voice and choice are integral to Mrs. Hubler's classroom culture. Students are actively involved in decision making, from selecting their learning activities to setting classroom goals. The sense of ownership fosters engagement and empowers students to take responsibility for their learning. Students are excited to share their learning with one another, their family members, and adults who walk into the classroom.

In this scenario, strategic seating arrangements are combined with flexible student options and visual aids integrated into the learning process. This approach empowers students to actively engage in their education in a highly personalized way, taking charge of their own path to success. Throughout this chapter, you will become equipped with personalized learning tools to help create a classroom that provides voice and choice for your learners while keeping learning at the forefront.

Teacher Self-Awareness Check

To begin your exploration of this topic, use the questions in this section to examine your teaching approach, classroom environments, and student interactions. Through this reflection, honestly observe your own strengths and areas for improvement as you seek to make meaningful changes to enhance student engagement and learning outcomes in your classroom related to the use of personalized learning. (Visit **go.SolutionTree.com/instruction** to access reproducible versions of Teacher Self-Awareness Check sections in this book.)

Have you ever considered how many of your waking hours are spent at work and how many hours of the day students spend in your classroom? Take a minute to think about your learning environment, which impacts how students feel, learn, and interact with one another in your classroom.

- How do you feel when you walk into your classroom?
- Is the classroom welcoming and inviting?
- Are you aware of how your students prefer to learn, and are there different seating options available for them to choose from throughout the day?

_____
_____
_____
_____
_____

At your favorite coffee shop or restaurant, where do you choose to sit? Every space and seating option within these establishments has a purpose and accommodates the people occupying it.

- Do you choose the high table with tall chairs, surrounded by televisions and people; the comfy couch by the fireplace, where you can curl up and work; or the quiet booth in the corner, where you can have an intimate conversation?

- Are your decisions affected by your mood, whether you are there to work or to relax, or whether you are meeting someone or are alone?

_____

What seating options do students have in your classroom, or is the seating all the same? Just as you have options at your favorite coffee shop or restaurant, students deserve options in the classroom that will accommodate their approach to learning.

- In general, what types of learning tasks do you ask students to complete throughout the school day, and how might your learning spaces better accommodate those tasks?

- If you were to revise your classroom's arrangement to realize the potential within its four walls, how might you arrange the furniture so it better aligns with the purpose of learning in your classroom?

_____

Personalized Learning Environments

Personalized learning encompasses a range of educational approaches that tailor instruction to each student's unique strengths, needs, and learning preferences. Michael B. Horn and Heather Staker (2015) of the Christensen Institute explain that traditional school models worked well during the 20th century's industrialization era, when the goal was to standardize teaching and learning so that graduates could take industrial jobs in factories. Those models don't meet the needs of 21st century students graduating into careers requiring knowledge and problem-solving skills. A personalized learning environment shifts from the traditional classroom environment of the one-size-fits-all model and embraces the notion that students have different learning preferences, from where they sit to how they learn. Students progress at different paces through different learning pathways. When students can move around and choose where they want to work, they are more likely to be comfortable, focused, and engaged. Providing students with options and creating systems where they need to choose various options from week to week will also stretch students out of their comfort zones while still ensuring they feel in control of the path they select.

In her book *Doable Differentiation*, Jane A. G. Kise (2021) provides the following research-based reasons why choice is a solid differentiation strategy.

- **Executive function:** Executive function encompasses skills like working memory, reasoning, information processing, task flexibility, problem solving, planning, and execution. These skills are fundamental to making choices. Students don't develop planning and problem-solving abilities by merely following instructions; they need to actively engage in processing information and making decisions. Providing students with choices allows them to practice and enhance these essential executive functioning skills.

- **Motivation:** Research identifies three main factors that motivate humans: (1) autonomy, (2) mastery, and (3) purpose. Offering choices fosters autonomy, which in turn increases intrinsic motivation. Angela Duckworth (2016) highlights that success requires both perseverance and passion. Passion often arises from a combination of self-efficacy and the autonomy to pursue personal interests or self-set goals. Thus, giving students choices not only supports their autonomy but also enhances their motivation and engagement. Students also are more likely to be interested in a learning activity if they feel they have some control and choice over how it is done, even if that begins with where they are sitting.

Later in this chapter, we write more about ways to personalize classroom learning environments, but as an initial vision, personalization of these environments often starts with having flexible seating arrangements within designated learning zones. According to special education teacher Chasity L. Hardin (2017), "With flexible seating, teachers are giving students the opportunity to learn about themselves and choose where they are better able to engage and participate in activities" (p. 7). Providing students with choices about where they work or seating options in specifically assigned areas gives them the space they need and engages them in the task at hand. Using flexible seating, teachers get to know their students better as individuals.

Let's take a closer look at why personalized learning environments are so important and then get into more specific details about implementing them in your classroom. Personalized learning environments are essential in today's educational landscape because they cater to the unique needs, strengths, and interests of each student. By moving classroom organization away from a one-size-fits-all approach, personalized learning promotes engagement, motivation, and a deeper understanding of the material. These environments acknowledge that every student learns differently and at their own pace, and they strive to provide the necessary resources and strategies to support individual growth.

Personalization is the cornerstone of our student-engaged framework; it ties all elements together. It is about creating a learning experience where students have voice and choice in their education, allowing them to take ownership of their learning journey. This approach fosters a sense of agency and empowerment, encouraging students to become active participants in their education. By integrating personalized learning, we can create a more dynamic, responsive, and inclusive classroom that adapts to the diverse needs of all learners. This high-level connection between personalization and our framework sets the stage for implementing specific strategies.

UNDERSTANDING WHY PERSONALIZED LEARNING ENVIRONMENTS ARE IMPORTANT

Sheninger (2021) explains that the right culture must be in place to create a learning environment conducive to unleashing the genius and talents of all students. Creating a personalized learning environment allows teachers to create a culture of curiosity, creativity, and collaboration where students feel valued and supported, enabling them to learn confidently. This is accomplished by addressing diverse classroom learning preferences, fostering intrinsic motivation (where internal rewards drive behavior), enhancing engagement, and supporting both physical and mental well-being through flexible learning spaces.

Flexible learning spaces also allow the facilitation of *sensory stimulation*, which is the activation of the sensory organs and neural pathways in the body, allowing the transmission of information to the brain. Researchers Stacy D. Thompson and Jill M. Raisor (2013) explain that the levels of sensory stimulation—sight, sound, touch, taste, and smell—are crucial for brain evolution. When students attempt to obtain information from their environments, they employ a host of neurological processes, including sensations from their bodies.

Being able to move and choose comfortable learning spaces positively impacts students' well-being. In her research, Jill M. Merritt (2014) explains that as physical activity increases, students' nervous systems become more stimulated and developed, counteracting the effects of prolonged sitting and inactivity experienced in school settings. This enhanced stimulation stems from the mind-body connection activated during learning. If students remain stationary, their proprioceptive (knowledge of the relative position of one's body) and kinesthetic (awareness of the movement of the body) senses are deprived of essential stimulation, leading to challenges in maintaining attention and focus, which can lead to stress and anxiety. When flexible seating is implemented, it can benefit students' overall sense of well-being. In his book *Brain Rules*, John Medina (2014) discusses how movement helps to increase blood flow to the brain and release endorphins, which, in turn, positively affects mood and cognitive function. Students who can move around the classroom and who have a choice in which seats are best for them are empowered to oversee their learning, decreasing the stressors of the physical environment.

Finally, the learning environment plays a key role in student engagement and behavior. As we established early in the book, disengaged students are more likely to perform at lower academic levels and exhibit problem behaviors in the classroom. A flexible learning environment can be a valuable tool for improving both student academic success and positive behaviors. For example, in their observation of classroom performance, researchers Molly E. Burgoyne and Caroline J. Ketcham (2015) found that stability balls, rather than the traditional classroom seating, increased on-task behavior among students. Without stability balls, 50 percent of student behavior they observed was on task, and 50 percent was classified as off task. However, when stability balls were introduced into the classroom, 85 percent of observed behavior was classified as on task, and only 15 percent was off task. When students had different seating options that incorporated movement, they could engage in the task because they felt safe and comfortable in the classroom.

IMPLEMENTING PERSONALIZED LEARNING ENVIRONMENTS

In our classrooms, we embrace a student-centered approach that fosters independence and engagement. Flexible seating arrangements allow each learner to choose their optimal workspace, whether it's a cozy reading nook or a collaborative pod. This freedom promotes comfort and focus, enhancing our students' ability to manage their own learning journey. Through the use of the Check, Check, Done! checklist, tailored to individual goals, students actively track their progress and take ownership of their tasks. This empowers them to prioritize, organize, and reflect on their work, nurturing a sense of responsibility and self-management. By creating student agency in every aspect of the classroom, from seating choices to daily tasks, we cultivate a learning environment where each student thrives and grows.

FLEXIBLE SEATING

As we've focused on throughout this chapter, using flexible seating rather than fixed desks and chairs caters to diverse learning preferences, promotes student engagement, and creates a more dynamic and adaptable learning environment. It encourages students to take ownership of their learning space, fostering a sense of autonomy.

Many seating options are available to help students be the most successful with assigned tasks. Seating options can include stability balls, wobble stools, scoop chairs, standing desks, lowered desks, and floor space. Flexible seating allows the classroom to go from a traditional, sterile classroom with desks in a row to one that incorporates student choice, improves student autonomy, and boosts engagement.

With flexible seating, students no longer have an assigned desk because they move through designated work areas and take their materials from station to station. Therefore, the culture of the classroom shifts because every student feels ownership over the entire classroom.

To begin implementing a flexible learning environment, you can start by using figure 2.1 (page 56) to assess your classroom's physical space and identify areas where flexible seating options can be incorporated. Use it to take inventory of what you have in your classroom, such as desks, chairs, stools, and tables. Think about whether desks or tables could be lowered, allowing students to sit on the floor. Put desks together in groups of three or four so students can move around these desk groupings to create small collaborative groups. Designate areas within the classroom space for individual work, collaborative work, and work with technology.

Current Seating Option	Quantity	Location and How It Will Be Used	Seating Option Still Needed	Quantity	Location and How It Will Be Used
Desks and chairs	28	Eight desks for independent work will be placed around the room against the walls to provide more space. Six desks will be in a cluster to provide space for group work. Eight desks will be used in pairs for students to work collaboratively with one other person. Six desks will be used in trios for collaborative workspace.	Floor desks	8	These will be at the front of the room so students can grab a floor desk if they feel like sitting on the floor to work during independent time.
Trapezoid table	1	This is currently used for minilessons.	Standing desks	3	Students can have the option to stand while working or collaborating.
Stools	6	These are currently used for minilessons.	Kidney bean table	1	Minilessons can be more collaborative.

FIGURE 2.1: Flexible seating inventory sheet.

*Visit **go.SolutionTree.com/instruction** for a free reproducible version of this figure.*

Figure 2.2 provides examples of signs to post around the classroom at designated spots. These allow students to navigate the classroom and know where each station is located and what is expected there.

Minilesson
- ☑ Bring a pencil.
- ☑ Stay on task.

Independent Work
- ☑ Work by yourself.
- ☑ Remain quiet.
- ☑ Stay on task.

Collaboration
- ☑ Have an open mind.
- ☑ Use an inside voice.
- ☑ Use the disagreement chart if a problem arises.
- ☑ Stay on task.

Digital Content
- ☑ Have a device with headphones.
- ☑ Stay on task and on the website.

FIGURE 2.2: Visuals to post at designated learning stations.

As we wrote in the Role of Accountability section of chapter 1 (page 13), it's important for students to learn accountability, something that you can reinforce in personalized learning environments by providing students with a sense of ownership of the classroom space. Allow students to have a voice by making them active participants in developing rules for the different seating options. What does it look like when they appropriately use that type of seating? What does it look like when they do not use it appropriately? What happens if students don't follow the rules? These examples ensure that flexible seating will effectively support student learning.

Introduce a variety of seating options to the students, explaining the benefits of each and setting clear expectations for their use. Figure 2.3 (page 58) provides example flexible seating rules.

> **Flexible Seating Rules**
>
> 1. Choose a **WORKING SPOT** that helps you do your **BEST** → a **SMART SEAT**.
> 2. Use each seat the **RIGHT WAY**!
> 3. If a spot is **NOT WORKING** for you, **MOVE** to a spot where you can do your **BEST**!
> 4. Take care of the classroom supplies! **CLEAN UP** after yourself and others.
> 5. Your teacher can move **ANYONE** at **ANY TIME** if you don't follow the rules!

FIGURE 2.3: Flexible seating rules.

Students can pick their seating option for the day to see how it feels, what they like about it, and if they can work productively sitting there. Have students choose a different seating option the following day and reflect on their choices.

Another way to implement flexible seating is by having students choose a seating option depending on their learning content. For example, during literacy time, students can read on stability balls while others sit on the floor. When students switch to working on mathematics, they can sit at traditional desks because they need a flat surface or want to work in isolation.

Allowing students to experience various seating options helps them decide what feels and works best for their learning needs. Another strategy is to have seating options listed for students to pick from on a chart. Students can mark off their name next to the seating option they choose, showing you they have tried it out. To take it a step further, you can have students write down what they like and don't like about the seating options they've tried. Figure 2.4 is a template students can use for reflection when trying out flexible seating options.

Seating Option	Time	Likes	Dislikes
Standing desk	9:10–9:25 a.m.	I was able to stretch and move more.	I got tired of standing toward the end.
Wobble stool	9:25–9:40 a.m.	I could move around, and it was fun.	I got distracted by the stool.
Floor lap desk	9:40–9:55 a.m.	I loved it! I could sit how I wanted and move to different areas.	Nothing. I liked it all.

FIGURE 2.4: Flexible seating student reflection sheet.

*Visit **go.SolutionTree.com/instruction** for a free reproducible version of this figure.*

As you implement this strategy with your students, it is important to remember that you are the teacher, and you have the right to take away flexible seating if students are not using it correctly. For example, with designated learning areas, students are no longer tied to a specific desk, so you must ensure students are responsible for their materials as they work. To effect this, you might have students put their supplies in cubbies or filing drawers instead of in individual desks. This frees up desks for community workspaces and allows students to be mobile throughout the entire room.

Flexible seating is a tool within your classroom. Continue to provide guidance and support as needed for students until they are successful, and ask for student feedback on the seating arrangements to adjust as needed. Soon, you'll find this framework creates a positive community culture where students feel responsible for the entire classroom.

PERSONALIZATION OF THE FOUR STATIONS

As you'll recall, within the student-engaged framework, there are four different stations designated for student learning: (1) minilesson, (2) independent work, (3) collaboration, and (4) digital content. You will learn about each of these in greater depth throughout the remainder of this book. For now, let's focus on how the learning environment can support each of these learning stations.

The minilesson station requires seating that accommodates a small group of students working with the teacher. Depending on the task and the number of students within the group, the minilesson should be done at a table, on the carpet, or around a demonstration table, standing, while the teacher models. This location should be farthest from the collaboration station because students in that station will be talking and could distract the group from the explicit minilesson.

The independent work station will vary depending on the student, but most students will work independently. Seating during this station can depend on individual student preference, whether it's a desk with a chair, a stability ball, or a wobble seat. Students could use a lap desk on the floor, a beanbag, or a standing desk. There is a lot of flexibility within this learning station. Think about utilizing the space in the room. If students are working independently, does it matter if the desks are pushed up against the wall? This change could clear space for a more open-concept classroom and provide work areas for other stations.

The collaboration station requires the most collaborative space because it involves projects, research, and a variety of resources and materials. Clustered desks, lowered tables where students can sit on the floor and work, vertical whiteboards, and countertops are all options for group work areas.

The digital content station incorporates technology and collaboration. Whether you have enough laptops for all students or a limited number of computers or tablets in your classroom, students should work in the same area, collaborating and sharing technology tools and resources.

Self-Management and Student Agency

Self-management and student agency are both crucial for fostering successful and engaged learners, and classroom setups aligned with the student-engaged framework create spaces for students to learn self-management while receiving opportunities to promote their agency. But what makes these traits so important for learning within our framework?

Self-management is regulation of one's behavior, thoughts, and emotions to reach desired outcomes. It involves students' engagement in metacognition to monitor and regulate their emotions, behavior, and expectations. It is the process of organizing their time, monitoring progress, and making adjustments based on feedback and data. Another way to look at this concept is to review the definition from the Collaborative for Academic, Social, and Emotional Learning (CASEL, n.d.) framework, which says self-management is the ability to "manage one's emotions, thoughts, and behaviors effectively in different situations and to achieve goals and aspirations. This includes the capacities to delay gratification, manage stress, and feel motivation and agency to accomplish personal and collective goals."

Student agency is the concept that students can take control of their learning and make decisions that are in their best interest. This involves students' ability to identify their needs, set their goals, and take action to reach them. Students may choose their path, the order in which they want to complete activities, the pace, and the place in the room that allows optimal learning.

These two aspects of teaching and learning give students the ability to become more independent, develop their sense of autonomy, and take responsibility for their actions and decisions. Implementing self-management and student agency in the elementary classroom encourages students to become more involved in their own learning and better prepared for success in the future.

When educators consider ways to improve the school environment and, by extension, learning outcomes in the classroom, there is a temptation to focus on the actions of the adults in the building. As Sheninger (2021) argues:

> There is a great deal of talk about how many changes are being spearheaded for the betterment of students, but rarely are students themselves asked for their input or unique ideas. Schools need to work for our students, not the other way around. (p. 116)

He advocates for making student agency a central component of the school culture, empowering students to take an active role in their own learning. Combined with the ability of students to self-manage, this shift toward students in decision-making processes can enhance the overall educational experience and contribute to a more student-centered approach.

UNDERSTANDING SELF-MANAGEMENT AND STUDENT AGENCY

Self-management is essential to maximizing student success, as it can give students the tools and skills needed to reach and track their learning goals. Student agency is powerful because it can create a strong sense of ownership in the classroom, which can foster an environment in which students are more engaged, motivated, and independent in their learning. According to Sheninger (2021):

> If we are to improve learning, and ultimately, classroom-based outcomes, student agency should become a core component of the school culture. It's empowering kids to own their learning (and school) through greater autonomy. It is driven by voice, choice and advocacy. (p. 116)

In classrooms that implement the student-engaged framework, teachers focus on how students manage their work time and how that affects their behavior. For example, while the teacher provides direct, explicit instruction to a group of students, the rest of the class independently works through stations, making decisions by themselves about what activities they want to accomplish and in what order they want to accomplish them. It is imperative for students to be able to complete work tasks in a timely manner, self-managing their time without an adult standing over them or giving multiple reminders to focus on the work at hand.

In the following sections, we look at a pair of strategies for building students' ability to self-manage and demonstrate agency.

IMPLEMENTING PRACTICES FOR SELF-MANAGEMENT AND STUDENT AGENCY

For students to practice agency in the classroom and develop self-management skills, Renaissance Learning (2023) states they must be able and motivated to take initiative in their learning. However, this independence does not mean teachers are free to sit on the sidelines. Guidance from an instructor is essential as students choose their direction. This can come from helping students set and prioritize goals and providing them with the tools and strategies to stay on track with those goals. Through self-management, students can develop a greater sense of responsibility for their own actions and learn to make good decisions. Within student-engaged classrooms, teachers utilize a tool called the Check, Check, Done! checklist and a visual tool called a progression board.

CHECK, CHECK, DONE! CHECKLIST

Think for a minute about the number of lists we create as adults to accomplish tasks and get things done—both at work and at home. Holding oneself accountable as an adult to complete everyday tasks and remember things is a life skill that students should be learning at an early age. The Check, Check, Done! checklist helps students practice self-managing their time and empowers them to make choices about their learning. They know the tasks they need to complete within the given time frame, and they can choose which tasks they complete for that day. This checklist can be created for a single day, week, or unit.

As shown in figure 2.5, the Check, Check, Done! checklist serves several purposes in our learning environment. It is divided into four sections—one for each station—with tasks for each station. It is organized like this to make tasks intentional for each station. For example, under the Digital Content header, up to four activities may be listed: (1) watching a video, (2) dropping into a location, (3) going on a virtual field trip, and (4) researching using a specific platform. As students complete a task, they check it off on their own Check, Check, Done! checklist.

Check, Check, Done!
Literacy

Minilesson Station	
RI.4.3—I can explain events in a historical text, including what happened and why, based on specific information in the text.	
RI.4.4—I can determine the meaning of general academic and domain-specific words or phrases in a text.	
RF.4.4—I can read orally with accuracy, appropriate rate, and expression on successive readings.	
Sequence of events	

Digital Content Station	
Watch the video about the American Revolution.	
Watch the video on the Boston Massacre.	
Complete this Edpuzzle video on the Boston Tea Party.	
Finish previewing the CCD slideshow.	

Independent Work Station
Read your independent book.
Practice the fluency passage (Handout A) throughout the week by recording yourself reading on Seesaw. Take a picture of the passage before recording yourself.
Complete your online vocabulary chart for the following terms. # revolution # perspective # convinced # liberty
Listen to or read "Facts About the Boston Massacre." Write down three facts, and turn them in to the teacher.

Collaboration Station
Read books from the Epic! collection on the American Revolution.
Write down six facts to create a "Six Things You Should Know" poster about the American Revolution.
Create your "Six Things You Should Know" poster on a document, a slide, or poster paper.
Post your "Six Things You Should Know" poster on Seesaw.

Buddy: _____

Buddy: _____

Source for standard: NGA & CCSSO, 2010a.

FIGURE 2.5: Literacy Check, Check, Done! checklist with Brain, Buddy, Buddy. *Visit* **go.SolutionTree.com/instruction** *for a free reproducible version of this figure.*

As students work through tasks, they can self-rate how difficult the tasks were for them to complete using a color-coding system. By color-coding tasks, students can communicate to the teacher whether a task was too difficult to complete even with help (red), was challenging (yellow), or was independently done with ease (green). If a teacher sees a task marked red on a student's Check, Check, Done! checklist, they know that they need to pull the student to answer any questions about the task, or that more direct instruction might be needed.

Another option is for the teacher to assign a color for each day of the week so the teacher and students can easily see which tasks were completed on which day. For example:

- Monday is red
- Tuesday is orange
- Wednesday is yellow
- Thursday is green
- Friday is blue

At the end of the week, the teacher can reflect on the number of tasks each student finished and have conversations with students who didn't complete their work about why they didn't. These discussions may show trends in type of task, day of the week, or specific station that provide the teacher and student with more information about the why behind task completion.

To begin using the Check, Check, Done! checklist, first decide the necessary activities for the week and then organize them within the four different stations. What direct instruction do you want to provide at a minilesson? What pieces will students practice during the independent work station? Is there a project they can create at the collaboration station? Are there videos you could utilize at the digital content station to increase background knowledge about the content you are teaching for the week? Once you have mapped out your activities, you will place them in their designated areas on the Check, Check, Done! checklist.

After you finish that, you can create a short video and share your screen to walk your students through the tasks at each station for the week. Making this video means students can rewatch it if they have questions while at the various stations; also, if any students are out sick, watching the video will help support them in catching up on what they missed in class. If you have a way to share the video with parents, it will help them understand their child's learning for the week, too.

It is important that you provide students with a paper copy along with a digital version of the checklist. If there are digital activities that require links, students must have access to a digital copy that houses the necessary hyperlinks for them to access. Students can access the digital version through a learning management system, website, or email. For younger students (grades K–2) or students who struggle to navigate these platforms, scanning a QR code that leads to the Check, Check, Done! checklist is also an option. If you are implementing a color-coding system, be clear on what the colors mean and how students will use them.

PROGRESSION BOARD

A progression board is a visual tool that helps students track their progress toward work completion or a learning goal. The progression board can be on a chart, poster, whiteboard, or SMART Board somewhere in the room where students can easily access it. Figure 2.6 and figure 2.7 provide examples of what these boards look like in the classroom. Each student has an item, similar to a game piece, that they will move around the progression board. Some example items for students include playing cards, numbers, magnets, index cards, pictures of themselves, or characters. All students begin in the same area and will move at different paces through the progression board.

Start	1	2	3
Zaria			
Kaden			
Alora			
Taryn			
Jaxon			
Elara			
Bryson			
Keenan			
Mylah			
Zayden			
Liora			
Seraphina			

FIGURE 2.6: Progression board—Example 1.

Start	Activity 1	Activity 2	Activity 3

FIGURE 2.7: Progression board—Example 2.

The board is divided into sections, each representing a task. As the student completes an activity and checks it off their Check, Check, Done! checklist, they move their game piece on to the next section. The progression board allows students to work at their own pace while visually representing where they are with task completion.

The board can be utilized as a communication tool as well. If the board is split with a horizontal line, the space below the line can indicate that a student has a question. Once a student has moved their piece below the line, they will move on to a task they can work on without teacher guidance until the teacher is able to answer their question. Once the student has no more questions, they move their game piece back above the horizontal question line. This allows students to continue working without interrupting the teacher while they are busy. When the teacher is available, they can assist students.

Conclusion

After reading through the first part of this book, you now have practical strategies for empowering students to take ownership of their learning journey through voice and choice. By combining verbal, nonverbal, and visual communication, educators can create a personalized and dynamic classroom environment that fosters growth, relationships, and self-awareness within students.

As you implement these strategies, use the provided Check, Check, Done! checklist shown in figure 2.8 to help guide you with your classroom transformation. Just like with your students, you have multiple pathways to achieve these goals in your classroom, so begin implementing what seems doable to you. Go at your own pace, and personalize the Check, Check, Done! checklist based on your classroom's needs. (See the appendix, page 141, for a blank version of this checklist.)

Check, Check, Done!

Foundations for Classroom Transformation

Communication	
Create your own conversation partners visual (see chapter 1, page 43).	
Post clear and visible learning goals for students to see.	
Create slides that help students manage their time and transition during stations (see chapter 1, page 35).	
Create visuals for students to use to help them navigate the room (refer to chapter 2, page 57).	

Relationships	
Set up your soft start structure, including directions and examples for soft start bins (see chapter 1, page 45).	
Schedule time for class meetings.	
Assign your students conversation partners. See figure 1.13 (page 45) for ideas to use in the classroom (for example, cookies and milk, chips and salsa, mac and cheese, and so on).	
Create and implement time for students to talk with their conversation partners.	
Learning Environment	
Take inventory of seating in your classroom (see figure 2.1, page 56).	
Create a personalized learning environment through flexible seating.	
Create designated locations for each of the stations, and create visual signs and expectations for those stations (see chapter 2, page 57).	
Create flexible seating rules as a class (see chapter 2, page 57). Hang these rules around your room for students to see daily.	
Accountability	
Create your own Brain, Buddy, Buddy visual (see figure 1.9, page 34). Assign students their buddies.	
Have students create a goal. Start with a fun one first and track their progress (refer to chapter 1, page 28).	
Create accountability buddy pairings for your students. Accountability buddies are used to track goals and progress on Check, Check, Done! checklists.	

FIGURE 2.8: Check, Check, Done! checklist to set the foundations for the student-engaged framework.

*Visit **go.SolutionTree.com/instruction** for a free reproducible version of this figure.*

PART 2

LEARNING STATIONS

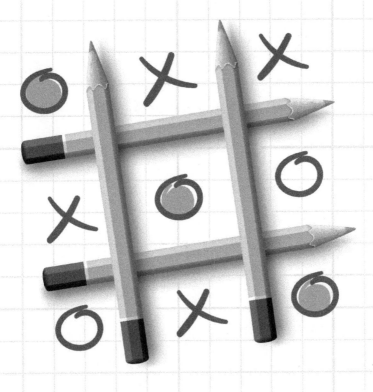

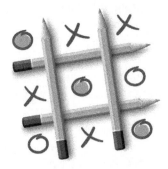

CHAPTER 3
MINILESSON STATION

Mr. Bean enters his third-grade classroom carrying a stack of books and articles, ready to engage his learners in a small-group minilesson. Today, he's teaching a lesson for standard RL.3.2, which states that students should be able to "recount stories, including fables, folktales, and myths" in a sequence of events (NGA & CCSSO, 2010a).

As a teacher renowned for his unique and engaging teaching strategies, he divides his class of twenty-five students into five groups, each with a mix of high, medium, and low readers. The students represent a range of academic levels, but Mr. Bean's intentionally differentiated lesson delivery ensures that all students are actively participating and making progress.

First, he provides low-floor questions accessible to all students: What is your favorite story? What is the story about? Who are the characters? and What happens in the story? Students immediately start a lively discussion on their favorite tales and are hooked. Mr. Bean encourages every student to share. The quick two-minute discussion wraps up as all students have shared their favorite story and are motivated to hear a new one.

He then reads the fable "The Tortoise and the Hare" in his animated voice paired with gestures, which captivates students. The students then practice skills aligned to the learning standard by accessing various pictures from the story and recounting the fable by placing the images in the correct order. Then, the

> *group members gather in smaller groups of two and three and take turns recounting the story after correctly ordering the images.*
>
> *Now that all students understand the standard, it is time that they practice with their own text. Mr. Bean hands each small group of students a different version of the same story, ensuring that the vocabulary and sentence structure are appropriate for their respective reading levels. He also gives them graphic organizers that each retell the story but look slightly different because they are leveled in difficulty. The first has boxes and pictures to match the story's order, similar to what the whole group practiced. The second has sentence stems with "in the beginning, middle, end" written at the top of boxes and a word bank. The third prompts students to recount the "Tortoise and the Hare" fable. Blank lines are provided for their responses. Mr. Bean differentiates in this way so he can understand whether students can master the standard at their personal reading level.*
>
> *By the end of the minilesson, all students have a good understanding of the standard, and they have had the opportunity to practice their reading comprehension and collaborative discussion skills. Mr. Bean can ensure all students, regardless of their academic level, engage in the lesson and make progress due to his differentiated instruction approach. Students are able to have academic conversations with any student in their class, which fosters a sense of community and confidence within each student. Once students understand the standard, he can help close the gap as they apply what they know and understand about the standard to other grade-level reading content.*

This scenario sets the stage for this chapter's exploration of minilessons within the broader instructional framework. Mr. Bean's example illustrates how a well-structured minilesson can effectively engage students at various academic levels through intentional differentiation and strategic grouping.

As part of the student-engaged framework, minilessons serve as a crucial component by providing targeted instruction that addresses specific learning standards. These lessons allow for flexibility and adaptability, ensuring that each student's needs are met through customized learning activities. This chapter guides you through the process of planning and executing minilessons, emphasizing the importance of aligning them with bigger instructional goals and standards. Additionally, we outline how to organize and integrate minilessons into a typical school week to ensure a balanced approach to instruction. This chapter also explores the use of grouping strategies to maximize student engagement and achievement.

As we dive into these topics, you will gain practical insights and strategies for implementing effective minilessons that enhance learning outcomes and create a collaborative classroom community. Although you can utilize these strategies for minilessons in any content area, the minilesson examples used in this chapter focus on literacy.

Teacher Self-Awareness Check

To begin your exploration of this topic, use the questions in this section to examine your teaching approach, classroom environments, and student interactions. Through this reflection, honestly observe your own strengths and areas for improvement as you seek to make meaningful changes to enhance student engagement and learning outcomes in your classroom related to the implementation of minilessons. (Visit **go.SolutionTree.com/instruction** to access reproducible versions of Teacher Self-Awareness Check sections in this book.)

Are you currently implementing small-group instruction?

What is your purpose in utilizing small groups?

What types of groupings do you currently use in your classroom?

Why do you group students in these ways?

Understanding the Minilesson Station

In the minilesson station, the teacher provides a short, focused instructional lesson to a small group of students. The explicit lesson empowers students to understand a specific standard or objective. Direct instruction is used as a structured teaching approach designed for students to master the specific skill or standard. According to Fisher and colleagues (2016) in their book *Visible Learning for Literacy*, direct instruction has a strong effect size of 0.59 relative to the average effect size in a year, which is 0.40.

Lessons are sequenced to build on one another, where first the students are learning together, until gradually they are practicing the skill with the group and finally they are independently assessed. The material is broken down into smaller steps throughout the week for explicit instruction. The direct instruction focuses on mastery, where students are clear on what skill, concept, or standard is being taught.

Key characteristics of an effective minilesson include the following.

- **Concise focus:** Minilessons zero in on a single learning objective or skill, making it easier for students to grasp and retain new information. This focus prevents cognitive overload and ensures that instructional time is used efficiently. By concentrating on one clear goal, teachers can provide more targeted instruction and feedback, helping students achieve mastery more quickly.
- **Efficiency:** Time is a critical factor in the classroom, and an efficient minilesson maximizes instructional minutes without wasting any. By being well prepared and staying on task, teachers can deliver powerful, focused lessons in a short amount of time. Efficient minilessons respect

students' attention spans and keep the pace brisk, which helps maintain engagement and motivation.

- **Engagement:** An engaging minilesson captures students' interest and encourages active participation. Techniques such as storytelling, questioning, and interactive activities draw students into the lesson and make learning more enjoyable. Engagement is crucial because it helps students connect with the material, deepening their understanding and retention of the content.
- **Scaffolds:** Providing scaffolds, such as visual aids, sentence starters, and graphic organizers, supports students' learning by breaking down complex tasks into manageable steps. Scaffolds are essential for helping students build on their prior knowledge and gradually develop new skills. By offering the right amount of support, teachers can guide students toward independence and confidence in their abilities.
- **Differentiation:** Recognizing and addressing the diverse needs of students is important to an effective minilesson. Differentiation involves tailoring instruction to meet the various readiness levels, interests, and learning styles within a classroom. This personalized approach ensures that all students, regardless of their starting point, can access the curriculum and make meaningful progress. Differentiation creates an inclusive environment where every student feels valued and supported.

Minilessons are explicit, and students should understand their objectives. Direct instruction with a small group allows for more in-depth exploration and ensures that all students gain a strong understanding of the content.

Minilessons are a flexible instructional tool; a teacher can use them to introduce new learning, reinforce skills, give students opportunities to practice with peers, or provide intervention for students who are struggling to gain proficiency with a standard. Research shows that small-group learning improves academic achievement, relationships with classmates, and psychological well-being (Johnson, Johnson, & Smith, 2014). When provided with focused, congruent lessons, students can learn complex learning objectives over time, making it more manageable for them to grasp new information and develop understanding.

These lessons are engaging and interactive and have a clear purpose that is driven by data obtained from independent tasks, digital content platforms, and in-class activities, while students know and understand the objective or standard that is the focus. Guide students throughout the lesson, and include opportunities for them to discuss with their peers, self-reflect, and apply what they've learned.

During a minilesson, all students learn the same content but may show their learning in different ways. Differentiation in this minilesson structure allows all students various avenues for demonstrating their understanding to ensure that every student can succeed without lowering the academic standards. In this approach, all students read the same story and participate in a discussion, creating a shared learning experience; however, the differentiation comes in how they show their comprehension.

For example, you might provide students with different types of graphic organizers tailored to their current individual ability levels. A student who needs more support might use a graphic organizer with guided questions and more structure to help them identify key elements of the story. In contrast, a student who is ready for an increased challenge might use an organizer that requires them to make inferences or connections to other texts.

This method does not mean that the expectations are lowered for any student. Instead, it ensures that every student is appropriately challenged and can demonstrate their understanding in a way that aligns with their current skill level and advances them to even higher proficiency. By differentiating the means of expression rather than the content, we are upholding high standards while providing equitable access to learning opportunities. This approach helps all students engage deeply with the material, enhancing their comprehension, communication, and critical thinking skills.

Small-group instruction is important because it allows all students personalized and accessible learning, purposeful differentiation, relationship building with peers and the teacher, facilitated collaboration, more immediate feedback, and a time when they have the teacher's full attention to ask questions. But the benefits to students go further. According to Avanti (2023), which is a personalized professional learning platform for teachers, the clarity and structure of direct instruction:

> are incredibly helpful for students with learning disabilities, many of whom may struggle with the organizing and processing of new information. Through a step-by-step approach with more repetition, reinforcement, and then opportunities for practice and review, tasks, assignments, or complex concepts are broken down into much more manageable pieces.
>
> Direct instruction also encourages active student engagement through frequent opportunities for student responding, practice, and feedback.

Having a small group of students with one teacher allows teachers to connect with students individually and facilitate questioning and discussion.

Often, when there is full-class questioning or discussion, not all students can participate. Fisher and colleagues (2016) state the importance of classroom discussion, showing it has a 0.82 effect size. Within a small group, all students can answer questions and share their thinking.

Also, students are less likely to disengage when in a small-group setting. According to Hattie (2023), the effect size of small-group learning is 0.46, larger than the average learning effect size of 0.40. This shows that having a small-group setting boosts students' confidence to participate, and it provides teachers greater flexibility to address individual student needs. As noted earlier, focusing on a small group of students for a designated time frame allows the teacher to differentiate for all students in the group, and students can take risks or ask questions while receiving immediate feedback, which, as we explore later in this chapter, is essential with any age group of students.

Deciding on the makeup of a small group is one of the teacher's most powerful decisions. In the *Journal of Direct Instruction*, Cathy L. Watkins and Timothy A. Slocum (2003) declare that small groups for direct instruction must be flexible and based on students' ongoing needs, writing:

> This flexible skill grouping based on students' instructional needs is very different from the practice of "tracking," in which students are assigned to rigid, inflexible groups based on general characteristics such as "intelligence." Tracking is absolutely incompatible with direct instruction because it does not allow for adjustment according to students' changing needs. (p. 87)

In the next section, we'll take a look at best practices for implementation, including more details about providing feedback and forming small groups.

Implementing Minilessons

Minilessons are brief, hence the name *mini*. Depending on students' ages, lessons are ten to twenty minutes. For students in kindergarten through second grade, minilessons should be around ten to fifteen minutes to match their attention spans. For students in third through fifth grade, minilessons can be slightly longer, around fifteen to twenty minutes. If lessons are longer than your students are capable of sustaining their attention for, engagement may dwindle, and you will not be able to facilitate as many groups.

Minilessons are designed with data in mind and are flexible, so students receive the instruction and support they need when needed. This means that teachers may adjust minilessons throughout the week depending on how the students are doing in regard to the standards being taught. Use classroom instruction and independent practice data to drive the minilessons. For example, if you are using a digital platform such as Khan Academy, Lexia, or ClassHero at the digital content station, you could also use these data to drive minilessons. Students who show they can complete a task independently may not need a minilesson that day.

During the minilesson, supports are in place so all students can access the content and apply the objective. Scaffolds are available to support students of all abilities, and differentiation occurs to meet the needs of individual students. For example, one student may have a graphic organizer with sentence stems, another may have a graphic organizer with a word bank, and another may have a blank graphic organizer.

In the following sections, we share guidance for providing effective feedback and structuring and planning for groups.

PROVIDE FEEDBACK

We mentioned previously that feedback is an essential part of minilessons conducted in small groups. It's designed so students can understand the expected learning outcome and where they are within the learning. According to Fisher and colleagues (2016), feedback has an effect size of 0.75, making it a highly impactful action.

To provide effective feedback, teachers must understand students' current level of performance, students' expected level of performance, and actions needed to close the gap. When teachers give feedback directly to students, their feedback also needs to be timely, specific, understandable to the student, and actionable. Fisher and colleagues (2016) write that feedback should be continuous and fall within four categories.

1. **Feedback about the task:** How well has the task been performed?
2. **Feedback about the process:** What strategies are needed to perform the task effectively?
3. **Feedback about self-regulation:** What knowledge and understanding does the student need in order to monitor and adjust their approach so they know what they're doing?
4. **Feedback about self:** How does the student evaluate their performance and feelings about the task?

When students are given feedback they understand, they can take action.

DETERMINE GROUP STRUCTURE

Several kinds of groups can be utilized in minilessons: homogeneous, heterogeneous, random, and flexible. Let's look at each.

HOMOGENEOUS

Homogeneous groups are groupings of like ability. Students in these groups have tailored instruction designed at their level. This grouping type works best for academic intervention, where students have proficiency gaps and need support to bridge them. To maximize the impact of intervention efforts, we recommend schools adopt a building-wide tiered system for intervention, such as response to intervention (RTI), for which there is strong evidence of effectiveness (Mattos et al., 2025). Instruction for groups that need intervention is determined by diagnostic data that identify skill deficits. It begins with high-quality core instruction and universal screening at Tier 1, with students who are identified as in need of academic or behavioral support receiving targeted intervention for grade-level skills with like-ability peers who need the same support (Tier 2). (Tier 3 is reserved for students who are missing foundational prerequisite skills and need intensive support from a dedicated intervention team to raise them up to grade-level proficiency.)

According to Hattie (2021), providing intervention to students in need of support has an effect size of 1.29, which is *massive*. As small-group direct instruction is implemented, progress monitoring supplies teachers with data and tools to track learning and growth. Intervention in small groups is a proactive approach to help ensure all students receive the support needed to succeed.

HETEROGENEOUS

Whereas homogeneous groups consist of students with similar abilities, *heterogeneous groupings* consist of students with different ability levels, learning preferences, or backgrounds. When students are placed in homogeneous groups from an early age, they can quickly become aware of which groups are considered the "smart kids" and which are seen as the "strugglers," which has a negative impact on self-esteem and motivation. Even when teachers make a good-faith effort to avoid divisive labels—for example, by using group names like the Lions, Tigers, and Bears—we find that students still recognize these distinctions. In contrast, heterogeneous groups might pair the highest performer with the lowest performer on a given standard, promoting collaboration and communication. This approach creates a sense of community in the classroom, where all students feel they belong and are valued. It encourages mutual support and learning, helping students appreciate diverse perspectives and abilities. We find this is also true of random groupings, which we discuss in the next section, with students feeling they are valued and belong because they are not strategically placed based on their similar abilities.

RANDOM

Random groupings are created visibly, in real time, where students can see that the selection is completely random. Thus, there are no proficiency-related labels and no reason for any student to feel devalued based on their grouping. Both random and heterogeneous groups build confidence within students, as they can have academic conversations with anyone in the class. Some of these students have never even been in a small group together because they have been labeled the "high kids" or the "low kids" since kindergarten; they have not received the opportunity to learn from one another or the supports to be able to participate together. Structuring grouping in this way is important for promoting a positive classroom environment where all students feel they are worthy and valued, no matter who they are with.

FLEXIBLE

Flexible groupings are a way to provide choice for students, reflective of their current learning needs. Writing for Edutopia, Andrew Miller (2020) states there are instances when:

> students should not simply be told that they will be receiving small group instruction; instead, the teacher should collaborate with students to leverage them as agents in their learning. Using effective self-assessment practices and reflective metacognitive strategies, students can take ownership in determining whether they need small group support.

To give students this choice, teachers can simply be available for support at the minilesson station on an as-needed basis. Giving students a choice to complete a task independently, with a partner, or at the station where the teacher can support learning is a flexible, responsive way to meet students' learning needs. In a fourth-grade literacy lesson we witnessed, the teacher began by having students discuss the conflict in a story with a partner. Then, partners shared ideas with the whole class. For the first activity, partners collaborated to match conflicts and resolutions while the teacher walked around, listening to conversations and gathering information on students' current knowledge. The whole group shared conflicts and resolutions, and the learning was synthesized for students. When the second activity was introduced, students had the opportunity to work independently, with a partner, or at the station with the teacher to receive more support. The teacher was prepared to teach the concept through a specific text but was unaware of who would choose this support.

Although this format of grouping for small-group instruction places the responsibility onto students, it should not be utilized all the time. One can see the downfalls of students not getting support when needed due to false confidence in their ability or lack of effort. Teachers will need to track patterns and analyze performance data to see if students receive and accept the appropriate support for instruction.

PLAN FOR GROUPING AND MINILESSON INSTRUCTION

The following four-step planning method is based on implementing random or heterogeneous groups where minilessons are structured so that each day builds on the day before. This is not the only way to utilize minilessons, as you may use them for intervention or flexible direct instruction where students choose the support they need for a specific skill. With heterogeneous groups, skills can change throughout the day or over the week to provide students with the necessary lessons.

STEP 1: DETERMINE YOUR CONTENT OR STANDARD FOCUS FOR THE WEEK

Choose a focus for the students to master, whether this be a specific skill, idea, or standard. What do you want students to master that may be challenging during whole-group instruction? This should be your focus for minilessons so students can receive explicit instruction in a small-group setting.

STEP 2: DECIDE HOW YOU WILL GROUP YOUR STUDENTS FOR THE WEEK

Consider using one of the following strategies to select groups.

- Do you have data indicating students are struggling or falling behind with one or more essential standards, signifying a need for intervention? If so, place students in homogeneous groups based on the reteaching and extension needs of the students. (See the discussion about homogeneous groups and intervention earlier in this chapter.)
- Are you teaching a new concept that all students need to learn? Group students heterogeneously. To group students heterogeneously, you want to mix highly proficient, proficient, and non-proficient learners for one or more standards to allow students to learn from each other and work with students they may not normally get to work with. Additionally, if you have students who show leadership skills, try to disperse them across several groups, as they can often help lead and keep the groups on task.

- Are students struggling with a skill, engagement, or motivation and need an internal boost? Utilize visible random groups. As noted earlier, random groups are created in real time in front of students so students know they are random. In his book *Building Thinking Classrooms in Mathematics, Grades K–12*, Peter Liljedahl (2021) suggests using playing cards to facilitate group assignments, "labeling each table (or desk) group with a card rank (2, 7, jack, queen, etc.) and having students draw a card from a deck to determine what group they would be in and where they would sit" (p. 44). Another way to randomize student groups is a random wheel or group generator. Knowing that groupings are random increases students' self-worth and takes away any labels of "high," "low," "leader," and so on.

STEP 3: PREPARE ACCESSIBLE, SCAFFOLDED, AND DIFFERENTIATED INSTRUCTION

As with all instruction, accommodations and modifications need to be in place so all students, regardless of their current proficiency with one or more standards, can contribute and learn within the small group, even though their current ability levels may look drastically different.

With small groups, we can readily differentiate the instruction and the type of assessment we give. One way to do this is through the use of graphic organizers. For example, let's suppose the focus of the minilesson is to master the following two standards:

> Recount stories, including fables, folktales, and myths from diverse cultures; determine the central message, lesson, or moral and explain how it is conveyed through key details in the text. (RL.3.2; NGA & CCSSO, 2010a)
>
> Compare and contrast the themes, settings, and plots of stories written by the same author about the same or similar characters. (RL.3.9; NGA & CCSSO, 2010a)

All the students could read the same story with guidance and show their learning through a graphic organizer. However, rather than everyone completing the same graphic organizer, different students would receive different graphic organizers, depending on their needs. Therefore, all students learn the same standard, but how they show their learning looks slightly different.

For example, figure 3.1 is a plot chart, which involves students writing the main events of the story's plot and then determining the moral of the story and comparing and contrasting several story elements. Because there is not much support for this graphic organizer, it is usually given to more proficient learners.

Recount Stories and Compare and Contrast Assessment

Standards:

RL.3.2—Recount stories, including fables, folktales, and myths from diverse cultures; determine the central message, lesson, or moral and explain how it is conveyed through key details in the text.

RL.3.9—Compare and contrast the themes, settings, and plots of stories written by the same author about the same or similar characters.

Feedback: _____ Proficiency Score: _____

Name: _____ Date: _____

Book Title: _____ Author: _____

Directions: Retell the story using the plot chart. Then, answer the three questions. Use the back of the paper if needed.

```
                    ┌─────────────┐
                    │   Climax    │
                    │             │
                    └─────────────┘
         ┌─────────────┐     ┌─────────────┐
         │Rising Action│     │Falling Action│
         │             │     │             │
         └─────────────┘     └─────────────┘
    ┌─────────────┐               ┌─────────────┐
    │Introduction │               │ Resolution  │
    │             │               │             │
    └─────────────┘               └─────────────┘
```

Questions:

1. What is the moral of the story?

2. What evidence do you have to support that?

3. Compare and contrast the settings, themes, and plots of _____ and _____.

Source for standard: NGA & CCSSO, 2010a.

FIGURE 3.1: Plot chart graphic organizer.

Figure 3.2 is a stoplight graphic organizer in which students take notes about the main ideas and details on the corresponding lines. (Here, the shaded areas at the top and bottom are green, the left side is lined in red, and the right side is lined in yellow.) They then fill out a Venn diagram to help them answer the last question on the stoplight graphic organizer.

Recount Stories and Compare and Contrast Assessment

Standards:

RL.3.2—Recount stories, including fables, folktales, and myths from diverse cultures; determine the central message, lesson, or moral and explain how it is conveyed through key details in the text.

RL.3.9—Compare and contrast the themes, settings, and plots of stories written by the same author about the same or similar characters.

Feedback: _____ Proficiency Score: _____

Directions: Retell _____ using the stoplight organizer. Write your introduction in the green area at the top of the organizer. On the red (left) side, write your main ideas. On the yellow (right) side, add details that support your main ideas. Use the green area at the bottom to write your conclusion.

Introduction (thesis):

Conclusion:

1. What is the lesson of the story? How do you know?
2. Compare and contrast _____ with _____ using the Venn diagram. (Compare and contrast at least two: setting, theme, and plot.)

Compare and Contrast

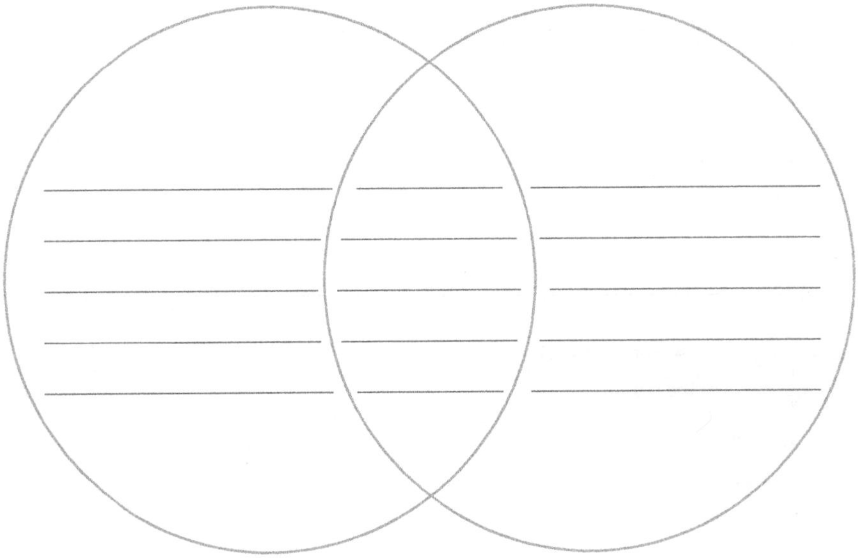

Source for standard: NGA & CCSSO, 2010a.

FIGURE 3.2: Stoplight and compare and contrast graphic organizers.

Figure 3.3 is the most straightforward graphic organizer for recording the plot, using the *beginning*, *middle*, and *end* language. Students then fill out the Venn diagram that includes write-on lines and the words *same* and *different* to provide the most support of all the graphic organizers shown here.

Recount Stories and Compare and Contrast Assessment

Standards:

RL.3.2—Recount stories, including fables, folktales, and myths from diverse cultures; determine the central message, lesson, or moral and explain how it is conveyed through key details in the text.

RL.3.9—Compare and contrast the themes, settings, and plots of stories written by the same author about the same or similar characters.

Feedback: _____ Proficiency Score: _____

Source for standard: NGA & CCSSO, 2010a.

FIGURE 3.3: Beginning, middle, and end and Venn diagram graphic organizers.

continued ▶

Directions:

1. Retell _____ using the following boxes.

   Beginning:

   Middle:

   End:

2. What is the lesson of the story?

   The lesson of the story is:

   _____
   _____
   _____

3. Compare and contrast _____ with _____ using the Venn diagram. (Compare and contrast at least two: setting, theme, and plot.)

Compare and Contrast

Different | Same | Different

If you have students who are in need of Tier 3 intervention (lacking foundational prerequisite skills for the grade level, as described earlier in the chapter), including students who may have an individualized education plan (IEP), it's vital to recognize that these students should *never* lose access to your grade-level instruction. As these students receive dedicated intervention, supply them with highly scaffolded materials that give them that grade-level access. With the third-grade examples shown in this section, students who are far behind a third-grade level could use a resource like Newsela (https://newsela.com), where you can utilize the same text and provide it at a lower reading level. Another option might be to have students listen to a recording of the text. Many tools, including generative AI like ChatGPT (https://chatgpt.com) or Google Gemini (https://gemini.google.com), can alter text levels or create organizers dependent on the level of students, which would help support learners within the group.

STEP 4: DETERMINE CONTENT FOR THE WEEK

Recall that minilesson content is a progression throughout the week that generally aligns with the following high-level steps.

- **Monday:** Students are introduced to the focus and collectively learn.
- **Tuesday:** Students revisit Monday's learning and begin to practice through teacher guidance.
- **Wednesday:** Students practice independently within the group and have collaborative conversations.
- **Thursday:** Students are assessed to gauge their understanding and application of the week's focus. These assessments are typically formative, designed to inform both the teacher and the student about the level of understanding achieved and to guide further instruction.
- **Friday:** Students who have not mastered the focus are provided more individual direct instruction, while the students who have mastered the focus utilize this time to work at a station other than the minilesson station.

Figure 3.4 (page 88) is an example of a five-day planning template with a completed plan, showing how you could move through a progressive minilesson week with heterogeneous or random groupings.

Monday	Tuesday	Wednesday	Thursday	Friday
Introduce the focus for the week. Guide students through the learning.	Revisit learning from Monday. Begin guided practice.	Practice independently with collaborative discussions.	Assess students in the focus area.	Provide direct instruction for students who still need support based on the data.
Focus: **RL.3.2**—Recount stories, including fables, folktales, and myths from diverse cultures; determine the central message, lesson, or moral and explain how it is conveyed through key details in the text. **RL.3.9**—Compare and contrast the themes, settings, and plots of stories written by the same author about the same or similar characters. Read or listen to the original "Cinderella" with a partner, independently, or as a whole small group. Focus on the story's central message and what details portray this by filling out a graphic organizer.	**Focus:** Revisit the graphic organizer together. Have students practice by completing the same graphic organizer with the story "The Rough-Face Girl."	**Focus:** Have students compare similarities and differences from the two stories on their own. Then, have a collaborative discussion.	**Focus:** Provide students with one of the **RL.3.2** and **RL.3.9** graphic organizers. Have them complete the organizer with the story "Ye Xian," comparing that story to the original "Cinderella." (Differentiation: Students could read on their own, they could listen to the story, or the teacher could read aloud if needed.)	**Focus:** Allow students who have mastered the standards to work on another station's tasks while students who need extra support can meet with the teacher in a minilesson where they receive direct instruction for what they need.

Source for standard: NGA & CCSSO, 2010a.

FIGURE 3.4: Minilesson planning template.

*Visit **go.SolutionTree.com/instruction** for a free reproducible version of this figure.*

Conclusion

This chapter explored the efficacy of minilessons as a powerful instructional strategy within the context of the student-engaged framework. As evidenced by research, including key findings from *Visible Learning for Literacy* (Fisher et al., 2016), minilessons provide a robust mechanism for improving academic outcomes through direct instruction in a small-group setting. The strategic sequencing from guided to independent practice ensures that students not only acquire but also master the content, preparing them for the subsequent challenges of independent learning.

Minilessons serve as a foundational tool in our framework, offering a versatile approach to introducing new concepts, reinforcing skills, facilitating meaningful peer interactions, and providing targeted interventions. Beyond academic gains, this approach creates a supportive and engaging learning environment that promotes psychological well-being and strengthens student relationships.

Looking ahead, the transition from structured minilessons to independent work stations represents a critical shift in our instructional framework. In the next chapter, we dive into the design and implementation of independent work stations that allow students to apply their learning autonomously. The progression from guided to independent activities is pivotal in cultivating empowered learners who are equipped to navigate the challenges of academic pursuits and beyond. The upcoming discussion not only outlines practical strategies for setting up effective stations but also highlights how to optimize these stations to reinforce the skills and knowledge gained through minilessons.

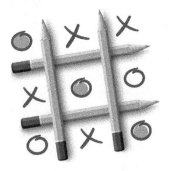

CHAPTER 4
INDEPENDENT WORK STATION

During whole-group direct instruction in Mr. Hutchins's first-grade classroom, students are learning how to blend, segment, and read short-vowel words with blends and digraphs. This week, they are focusing on the digraph ch in core instruction.

The independent work station looks different for all students in the classroom. Gianna can identify all upper- and lowercase letters but only knows thirteen sounds. During the independent work station, she may watch a video online that reviews all letter sounds, do an activity in which she sorts pictures by their initial sound, listen to a recording of the teacher saying a sound while she writes the letter that represents that sound on a whiteboard, or say the letter sounds while her student support teacher holds up grapheme cards. These independent activities were collaboratively planned by Mr. Hutchins and Gianna's student support teacher, Mr. Brooks. Once a week, Mr. Brooks records which letter sounds Gianna gets correct and which sounds she says incorrectly.

Olivia, another first-grade student, can accurately blend words with digraphs and fluently reads approximately thirty words per minute. Although she is accurate, she has set a goal to read more fluently at a higher rate. At the independent work station, she can choose to play a game of matching digraphs to pictures with initial or final sounds representing the digraphs. She may repeatedly read decodable books from her book box. Her teacher has also recorded himself reading word chains for her to write them on a whiteboard

> *to practice phoneme-grapheme mappings of closed-syllable, multisyllabic words. Twice a week, she records herself reading a passage that aligns with the weekly phonics skill, listens to herself, and reflects on her fluency progress.*
>
> *Robert accurately and fluently reads one hundred words per minute. He has passed the phonemic awareness and phonics diagnostics and already knows most vowel teams, which have not yet been taught in core instruction. At the independent work station, he focuses on first-grade comprehension standards to better understand his reading. He can choose to review and play the digraph matching game and practice phoneme-grapheme mapping of multisyllabic words. Mr. Hutchins has also created some graphic organizers focused on helping students retell stories (including the central message) and describe characters and major events; Robert fills these out while reading.*
>
> *All three students may choose from these independent learning options listed in their Check, Check, Done! checklists throughout the week. For students who are out of the room for reading or additional support and have limited independent work time, Mr. Hutchins highlights tasks that they must complete each day. After completing the assigned task, students can choose what they want to complete if they have additional work time.*

As this scenario illustrates, this chapter emphasizes personalized learning as a critical component of the student-engaged framework for how it ensures teachers meet students where they are in their learning. The organization of the independent work station (not workstation) across a typical school week showcases the balance between structured guidance and student autonomy. By providing a variety of targeted activities and allowing students to make choices about their learning, you can create an environment that encourages both skill development and independent problem solving.

In this chapter, we explore how teachers design and implement differentiated independent work stations, specifically tailoring learning activities to meet diverse student needs. We dive into strategies used to support various ability levels in all content areas so you gain insights into effective methods to engage all students. Use this chapter as a practical guide to implement similar differentiated instructional strategies in your own classroom, highlighting the impact of thoughtful, responsive teaching on student engagement and achievement.

Teacher Self-Awareness Check

To begin your exploration of this topic, use the questions in this section to examine your teaching approach, classroom environments, and student interactions.

Through this reflection, honestly observe your own strengths and areas for improvement as you seek to make meaningful changes to enhance student engagement and learning outcomes in your classroom related to independent learning. (Visit **go.SolutionTree.com/instruction** to access reproducible versions of Teacher Self-Awareness Check sections in this book.)

When you directly teach a group of students during minilesson instruction, what is the rest of your class doing during this time?

_____
_____
_____
_____
_____

Are students self-sufficient, engaged, and working independently on challenging and motivating tasks?

_____
_____
_____
_____
_____

Can students navigate the learning environment, access materials, and accomplish assigned tasks?

_____
_____
_____
_____
_____

Do students understand the purpose behind their learning?

_____
_____
_____
_____
_____

Are tasks relevant to them?

_____
_____
_____
_____
_____

Understanding the Independent Work Station

At the independent work station, students are expected to independently work on tasks that align with and are tailored to their learning needs. Independent instruction looks different from direct instruction because students are their own teachers. This paradigm change shifts responsibility and expertise from an adult teacher modeling content and guiding practice with immediate feedback to a student doing application and purposeful practice. Independent work should align with direct instruction students receive from the teacher. As Robert Marzano (2019) states:

> When students are learning a new skill or process, the teacher first provides a clear demonstration of it. After this demonstration, students should have frequent opportunities to practice discrete elements of the skill or process as a whole in situations where they have a high probability of success. (p. 67)

Independent learning practice should parallel skills students have already learned in direct instruction, including instruction via the minilesson station, and ensure that tasks are both challenging and manageable. Such an approach embodies a series of aligned and research-backed concepts.

- **Productive struggle:** In this state, students engage with tasks that are sufficiently challenging yet achievable with effort, leading to greater engagement and learning efficacy, as these tasks require students to apply and extend their existing knowledge and skills in new and meaningful ways (Blackburn, 2018).
- **Zone of proximal development:** This suggests that optimal learning occurs when tasks fall within the range of what a student can do with and without help (Shabani, Khatib, & Ebadi, 2010; Vygotsky, 1978).
- **Desirable difficulty:** This explains that appropriately challenging tasks enhance long-term retention and understanding (Bjork & Bjork, 2014; Bjork Learning and Forgetting Lab, n.d.).

Students who have questions or need support rely on each other through the Brain, Buddy, Buddy system (see Brain, Buddy, Buddy, page 33, in chapter 1). Teachers' sole focus during this station is giving direct instruction to small groups, not interrupting instruction to answer questions that a peer can answer for students working independently.

Teachers should never use independent work to fill time or keep students occupied with busywork. They can utilize a variety of highly effective tasks and practices to maximize this time and build student knowledge and skill mastery. Workstation time should be intentionally planned and thoroughly thought out to provide opportunities for students to apply new information, practice skills, and demonstrate their mastery of standards on their own. According to educational consultant Suzy Pepper Rollins (2014), "Effective student work sessions are characterized by increased student control (and a concomitant increase in personal accountability), high levels of student engagement, visible demonstration of student thinking, and a reliance on cooperative learning" (p. 96). While working independently, students have ownership of their learning, and according to Fisher and colleagues (2016), students must be empowered to ask and answer three questions about each lesson.

1. **What am I learning today?** This question requires a deep understanding of the concept of *learning intentions* (*learning objectives*), which are clear statements (phrased in student-friendly language) that define what students are expected to learn by the end of a lesson or unit. By explaining learning intentions at the start of each session, teachers enhance transparency and align student expectations with learning goals.
2. **Why am I learning this?** This question is about *relevance* and connects to students' existing knowledge, experiences, or future intentions. When students understand why what they are learning matters, especially

when the learning is connected to real-world concepts and challenges of interest to them, their motivation and engagement increase significantly.

3. **How will I know that I learned it?** This question directly links to the concept of *success criteria*, benchmarks that indicate whether and how well students have achieved the learning intentions. These criteria are vital to teachers and students because they provide a clear road map for assessing progress and achievement. Success criteria should be specific, measurable, and, like learning intentions, communicated to students at the start of the lesson so they know what they want to achieve and they are able to self-assess their progress toward those goals.

When independent work tasks are aligned to high learning standards and personalized to students through differentiation and scaffolding, students can deepen their learning, work toward mastery of skills, and build self-efficacy.

The key is strategically spacing learning opportunities throughout the day and week that connect and build on one another. Rishi Sriram (2020), associate professor at Baylor University's School of Education, states this about engaging students and getting the most out of independent work time: "Distributing practice evenly over time is one of the most helpful techniques for deepening learning. Because the brain can absorb only so much information at a time, students benefit more from frequent, shorter sessions than from longer ones."

To get to deeper levels of understanding, students need repetition and practice of surface-level skills until they become automatic. Once skills are mastered, brain space is freed up for more advanced learning. According to Fisher and colleagues (2016):

> Students need to regularly have the occasion to rehearse what they have learned. We cannot overestimate the importance of this consolidation—in many senses, the purpose is to *overlearn* the surface knowing so that students can readily access the information when they move to the deeper, comprehension, and inferential tasks. (pp. 61–62)

For example, consider how a student learns to decode words with a specific digraph like *ch*. Initially, they might practice blending and segmenting words such as *chat*, *chip*, and *much* during direct instruction. To consolidate this knowledge, they repeatedly engage in activities like matching digraphs to pictures, reading decodable books featuring the *ch* digraph, and writing word chains that incorporate these sounds. Through consistent practice and reinforcement, students "overlearn" the basic skill of recognizing and pronouncing the digraph *ch*, which ensures they can effortlessly apply this knowledge in more complex reading and comprehension activities later on.

To deepen learning, students need opportunities and time to solidify their knowledge and build a solid foundation through repetition and practice. The independent work station should be structured so that students can feel confident completing assigned tasks. Students will succeed more when established routines encourage them to approach and attempt work—even if it is perceived as hard or challenging—and peers provide support and guidance systems. According to Fisher and colleagues (2016):

> Most of us are more likely to engage in difficult, complex, and risky learning if we know there is help nearby, that there are safety nets, [and] that we will not be ridiculed if we do not succeed—this is where the power of a teacher lies. (p. 25)

Teachers need to foster a learning environment that allows students to grow through trial and error, learn from their mistakes, and take risks in their learning. As students work to build these skills and grow toward mastery of content standards, they build their self-efficacy and belief in themselves as learners. Marzano (2019) describes this progression:

> Once students are comfortable with a skill or process and have experienced success with it in a wide range of situations, they engage in independent practice in which they focus on performing the skill or process skillfully, accurately, quickly, and automatically. (p. 68)

More opportunities to practice result in more honed skills. These skills become automatic, resulting in highly efficient performance. When students' performance is highly effective, their confidence is boosted. When students have high confidence in their learning ability, they become more invested and engaged in their work because they are responsible for everything they accomplish independently. Researcher and educational consultant Andy Hargreaves (2021) explains the benefits of students' hard work and achievement of mastery:

> Hard-earned accomplishment provides more lasting fulfillment and engagement than fleeting moments of fun. Mastery involves command of a knowledge or skill and the capacity to exercise self-control in the face of obstacles and setbacks. If you've ever been at the peak of your powers as a teacher, leader, artist, or athlete, you know what mastery feels like. (p. 31)

When the teacher shifts from directly instructing to facilitating learning, students take ownership of that learning. Pepper Rollins (2014) stresses the importance of intentionally organizing and aligning tasks so teachers put learning in the students' hands: "It's about content experts choreographing student work sessions in which students do more of the talking, the problem-solving, and the creating. During these periods, a significant amount of academic control (and accountability) shifts from our shoulders to theirs" (pp. 94–95).

The shift from direct instruction to a more student-centered approach, where learners take charge of their educational journeys, creates significant gains in both skill mastery and personal development. The role of the teacher evolves from a primary knowledge provider to a facilitator of learning, creating environments where students are at the forefront of inquiry and application. This empowering shift enhances students' autonomy, as well as enriches their learning experiences, preparing them to tackle challenges with resilience and creativity.

Implementing Independent Activities

If teachers intentionally align tasks to match the standards they have taught, students can maximize their learning with the independent work station. Initially, implementation seems simple. The teacher explicitly teaches a concept and assigns students tasks that allow them to practice it. However, learners are complex, and several factors affect each student's ability to successfully complete work on their own. The following strategies and practices guide teachers through planning, organizing, aligning, and implementing independent work tasks that meet individual learning needs and personalize learning for all students.

PROVIDE A CLEAR LEARNING PATH

To start planning independent activities, teachers need to understand what they want students to learn and be able to define and assess what it looks like if they've learned it. Understanding standards, defining what student proficiency with these standards looks like, and helping students set learning goals to progress toward mastery are all sound teaching practices that provide clarity and learning purpose.

Let's consider a fourth-grade learning intention: "Students will understand the phases of the water cycle and be able to identify each phase." A teacher might break this down into clear, actionable steps for planning independent activities by first defining what proficiency looks like. For this standard, that proficiency might include being able to label diagrams of the water cycle, explain each phase (in writing or verbally), and demonstrate understanding through a creative project, like constructing a model or simulating the water cycle.

Next, the teacher helps students set specific, measurable goals. For example, one goal could be to accurately label all parts of the water cycle on a diagram by the end of the week. Another goal might involve explaining the significance of each phase in their own words during a presentation.

Based on these goals, the teacher plans independent activities that align with the defined proficiency. For example, these could include the following.

- **Research task:** Students use classroom resources to find information about the water cycle, focusing on identifying key details about each phase.
- **Diagram labeling:** Students complete a worksheet or a Seesaw activity where they label parts of the water cycle using notes they have compiled from their research.
- **Creative project:** Students create a 3-D model demonstrating each phase of the water cycle and present their model to the class.

Finally, the teacher assesses students' diagrams, presentations, and projects to check for understanding and proficiency. Students also reflect on their learning, discussing what they found challenging and what they understood well. Providing work exemplars, models, and rubrics for students to compare their work can further help students self-assess and reflect on their progression toward proficiency.

This last point about self-assessment is key, as this practice has been shown to significantly impact learning by promoting students' ownership and awareness of their progress. According to *Student Self-Assessment* author Katie White (2022), engaging students in self-assessment helps them develop critical thinking skills and a deeper understanding of their learning process. This practice encourages students to take responsibility for their learning and become more motivated to achieve their goals.

For example, teachers can display student writing examples for each proficiency scale level or rubric score. Students can compare their own writing to each example and evaluate their work. This process not only helps students understand the standards they are aiming to meet but also allows them to identify specific areas for improvement and set targeted goals for their learning journey.

Another way students can evaluate themselves is by listening to recordings of someone reading text with various rates, expressions, and accuracy levels. These recordings can teach students the difference between fluent and emerging readers. Students can then record themselves reading, compare their recordings to the provided models, and determine their proficiency.

Providing examples of proficient work gives students a benchmark they can use as they work toward meeting a standard in manageable stages. Comparing and contrasting their work with examples helps define criteria that students have mastered and areas in which students are lacking and need to improve.

SET INDEPENDENT GOALS

Once students know their current level of understanding, they need to know what they must do to demonstrate proficiency with the standard. Building on the goal-setting strategies discussed in chapter 1 (page 28), this process motivates students by helping them take ownership of their learning. As Bryan Goodwin and Kristin Rouleau (2022) emphasize in their book *The New Classroom Instruction That Works*, committing to a personal learning goal is important, as it signals to our brains the importance of staying engaged. Evidence supports this, showing that personal goal setting significantly boosts student learning outcomes, as Goodwin and Rouleau (2022) state:

> To learn something, we must commit to learning it—often by setting and monitoring progress toward a personal goal that, in effect, reminds our brains to stay powered up. More than a dozen empirical studies, in fact, point to creating personal learning goals as a powerful strategy for improving student learning. (p. 85)

Understanding where students stand within learning progressions, a concept initially introduced in this chapter with the discussions of learning intentions, success criteria, and the overall framework of structured learning, helps teachers guide students toward appropriate goals. For example, in writing, a student may set a goal to enhance descriptive details by including at least three sentences with sensory detail in each assignment. In reading, a goal might be to improve reading speed by one word per minute each week.

When setting goals, students benefit from identifying at least two specific actions they will take to practice their goals. This dual action approach, grounded in research by Barry J. Zimmerman (2002), suggests that multiple simultaneous strategies enhance focus and provide alternative paths to mastering a skill, increasing the likelihood of success. For example, if students aim to improve their reading rate, they could commit to reading aloud twice daily and timing themselves to track progress. For writing, learning a new adjective each day to enrich their vocabulary could be an easy action to take.

Incorporating clear learning targets, as Marzano, Pickering, and Pollock (2001) propose, enables effective goal setting and self-reflection to adapt goals to students' personal needs. Feedback plays a critical role here, as it provides specific insights into what students are doing correctly and what needs improvement, which helps guide their progress toward these goals. Over time, students should be encouraged to monitor and self-evaluate their progress, using tools like proficiency scales, rubrics, and examples of student work to clearly visualize what is expected with learning targets.

PLAN RELEVANT LEARNING TASKS

Teachers must intentionally plan relevant learning tasks aligned with standards and build off students' prior knowledge and instruction. Sheninger (2021) declares, "Relevance should be non-negotiable in our learning task. If a student does not know why [they are] learning something, that is on us. Learning today and beyond must be personal for every student" (p. 57). Teachers need to know and understand their students as learners to personalize instruction.

Observations within whole-group and small-group direct instruction can also drive the tasks and activities students are assigned during their independent learning time. Remember, students will be working independently for most of the independent work station. Plan tasks that challenge students but can be done independently. Tasks must drive each student to do the work and think independently.

When planning tasks that challenge students yet remain independently doable, teachers should design activities that prompt cognitive engagement without being overwhelming. While worksheets often serve as go-to resources for this purpose, use them sparingly, as they may not always promote deep thinking, cognitive struggle, or problem-solving skills. Instead, tasks should be thoughtfully created to encourage independent thought and application of skills. Following are some examples of how these tasks might look.

- **Critical thinking tasks:** In English language arts, instead of offering a simple fill-in-the-blank worksheet on a reading passage, assign students to create a mind map that explores the themes and character relationships in the text. This encourages them to analyze information and synthesize it in a new, visually organized way. (Visit https://canva.com to find multiple examples of mind maps.)
- **Problem-solving tasks:** In mathematics, rather than handing out a page of repetitive calculation problems, consider tasks that require students to apply several steps to solve real-world problems. For example, students could calculate the total cost of ingredients needed to bake cookies for their class, adjusting the quantities and budget constraints.
- **Research projects:** In science, instead of having students answer questions from a textbook, have them conduct a small experiment or engage in a research project on local ecosystems, documenting their findings in a science report format.

To make sure that the tasks are appropriately challenging and not beyond the students' capability, use common formative assessments. These will help you identify each student's strengths and areas needing improvement and tailor tasks that target their specific developmental needs. If tasks are too difficult for students to complete on their own, or students don't have the skills necessary to complete the tasks, the students will practice them wrong. Even with well-designed tasks, some students may require occasional support. Implementing a structured support system like the Brain, Buddy, Buddy strategy discussed in chapter 1 (page 33) allows students to seek help from their internal resources or peers before turning to the teacher. This system encourages self-reliance and problem solving among peers but should be structured so the students are not too dependent on their classmates. It's important that the tasks are still primarily achievable through individual effort.

Teachers must continually monitor how students manage these tasks and make adjustments as necessary. Observing students during independent work and gathering feedback on their experiences can provide valuable insights into whether the tasks hit the mark or need refinement.

GIVE PERSONALIZED FEEDBACK

Keeping standards and expectations the same for everyone sets the bar high and ensures a guaranteed and viable curriculum for all (Marzano, Warrick, & Simms, 2014). But the learning path can look different based on students' individual needs, degree of background knowledge, and current proficiency level. Teachers must know where each student is and provide personalized feedback to help them progress.

Like in direct instruction, feedback must be prevalent for independent work, though it looks different when implemented as part of an independent work station. During independent work, feedback shifts from directive to more consultative, focusing on guiding students to reflect on their learning and identify areas for self-improvement. This type of feedback encourages greater student autonomy and responsibility for their learning outcomes. The following are some ways that feedback at this station is distinctive from feedback in direct instruction.

- **Feedback is delayed and detailed:** Unlike the immediate corrections consistent with direct instruction, feedback in independent settings may be delayed to allow students time to engage with the task and attempt to troubleshoot their own errors. When students receive feedback, it is detailed and provides insights into not just what was incorrect but why certain choices might lead to better outcomes.
- **Feedback focuses on metacognition:** Feedback during independent work often involves questions or prompts that encourage students to think about their thinking process. This can help them develop skills

in self-assessment and self-regulation. For example, after a writing task, instead of directly correcting grammar, a teacher might return the work with comments such as, "Can you find a stronger verb to convey the action here?" or "What could make this argument more persuasive?"

- **Feedback encourages peer review:** Independent work often incorporates peer feedback mechanisms where students learn to constructively critique each other's work. This not only builds critical thinking skills but also fosters a collaborative learning environment. For example, students may have prompts that help them provide feedback, such as, "I would like to hear more about . . ." or "I like _____, but I don't understand."
- **Feedback utilizes reflective practices:** Teachers might encourage students to write a brief reflection on their learning process, what strategies worked, what didn't, and how they plan to approach similar tasks in the future. This can be as simple as circling an emoji face, as in figure 4.1.

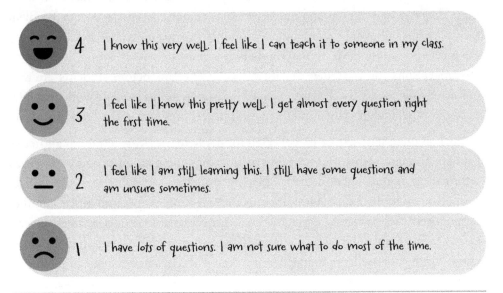

FIGURE 4.1: Simple emoji-based reflection worksheet for students.

Pepper Rollins (2014) says that, as work shifts from the teacher to the student, "it is paramount to monitor the quality of work and provide feedback that helps students advance toward the goal. This is the crucial time when students process and practice the standard" (p. 99). Because students usually work on their own, teachers must collect student learning evidence to hold them accountable for their practice. Being cognizant of what students are turning in and prioritizing what you collect helps you manage materials and ensure timely student feedback.

Be conscious of what you collect from students in the independent work station. This time is for practice; not every piece of work should be collected and evaluated. Collecting too much student work is overwhelming for teachers; you feel like you can't keep up, which compromises your ability to provide effective feedback. For example, a teacher might assign students several mathematics tasks to practice independently within any given lesson, but they might evaluate and grade just one problem according to the proficiency scale it aligns with.

As teachers, we want to work on giving quality feedback that is based on progress toward proficiency, not quantitative data that are surface level and don't tell students how to improve when they work independently. If a teacher assigns students a worksheet full of mathematics tasks and corrects every problem, the feedback they give to students likely includes the number of correct answers and a percentage. These quantitative data do not explain what was incorrect or why. A percentage of correct answers doesn't help students when solving future mathematics problems.

Contrast this with correcting just one problem. In this case, a teacher can analyze how each student attempted to solve it, find patterns, and look for misunderstandings. They can see who has and hasn't met the standard. Focusing on one problem is manageable, allowing the teacher to promptly provide corrective feedback. They can meet one-on-one with students and discuss where they went wrong, and address misconceptions the next day during direct instruction before students attempt problems independently. Teachers can also use anonymous student work examples to display and analyze correct mathematical procedures within the focus problem.

Much as quantitative data are collected for mathematics instruction, quantitative data are also collected for literacy instruction, but the data do not offer as much information as qualitative data do. Having students read some text and answer a series of multiple-choice questions can provide a quick glimpse at the number of questions they answered correctly, but a lot of variables can determine success in quantitative measures, which makes it hard to determine what students really know. Have your students independently read a text passage to collect qualitative data during literacy instruction. To assess their comprehension of the passage, have students complete and turn in a graphic organizer that aligns with a specific literacy standard. For example, students must often find the main idea when reading fiction texts. Figure 4.2 shows a graphic organizer aligned with a literacy standard that students can complete independently. This graphic organizer informs teachers of whether students can identify three supporting details, explain how the details support the main idea, and summarize the text. All components of the organizer cover the requirements of the fourth-grade literature standard RL.4.2: "Determine a theme of a story, drama, or poem from details in the text; summarize the text" (NGA & CCSSO, 2010a).

RL.4.2 Main Idea and Details Assessment

Text Title: _____

Name: _____

Detail:	Detail:	Detail:
How does this detail support the main idea of the text?	How does this detail support the main idea of the text?	How does this detail support the main idea of the text?

Main Idea:

Summarize the text.

Source for standard: NGA & CCSSO, 2010a.

FIGURE 4.2: Graphic organizer designed to collect data on student understanding of a literacy standard.

The graphic organizer could be broken down into small chunks for the students to complete and the teacher to analyze. Students may initially define the main idea and identify three key details that support it. Later, they could explain how the details support the main idea and summarize the text.

In literacy instruction, teachers can provide quality feedback using graphic organizers that align with all components of a standard. In the example in figure 4.2, a teacher can identify whether a student has met the standard by identifying the main idea, listing three details within the text, explaining how the details support the main idea, and summarizing the text. Quality feedback would include guiding students to complete each component of the graphic organizer. If a student can identify three details within the text but cannot explain how those details support or relate to the main idea, they are still approaching the standard. The teacher can suggest that students include more details in their summary to prove they comprehend what they just read. This feedback is more prescriptive and related to students' current knowledge and skill levels.

How students show their learning should vary as well. Opportunities to prove their learning through different modalities and to show their proficiency in multiple ways accommodate all learners. Differentiating assessments and adding performance tasks that require multiple pathways allow all learners to approach tasks and demonstrate a variety of skills.

UTILIZE THE CHECK, CHECK, DONE! CHECKLIST

To further tailor the independent work station for individual students, you can personalize the tasks listed in the Check, Check, Done! checklist to accommodate each student's needs. You can create independent tasks by collaborating with other instructors from reading support, special educational services, or English learner resources. Also, you can add tasks that align with the instruction students receive outside the classroom. Following are two examples of how you could implement this.

1. **Integrating reading support:** A student meets with a reading support teacher.
    a. *Checklist integration*—Collaborate with the reading support teacher to design tasks that reinforce reading strategies covered during support sessions.
    b. *Checklist tasks*—(1) Read a passage using a guided reading strategy, (2) highlight key words that end with *-ion*, and (3) summarize a passage in your own words on a response sheet or using Seesaw.

2. **Supporting English learners:** An English learner needs practice in language acquisition.
    a. *Checklist integration*—Coordinate with the English learner teacher to create tasks that supplement language lessons.
    b. *Checklist tasks*—(1) Watch a video related to the week's topic and list new vocabulary, (2) use new words in sentences or a short paragraph, and (3) discuss the topic with a peer or record a spoken summary, focusing on accurately using new vocabulary.

By allowing students to select and highlight which tasks they wish to tackle first from the Check, Check, Done! checklist, you empower them with choice, catering to their interests and learning preferences. This method prioritizes student agency and enhances engagement, as students feel more connected to and responsible for their learning.

Conclusion

This chapter on independent work stations dove into the core principles of fostering autonomy and responsibility in students' learning processes, a crucial aspect of the student-engaged framework. We've seen how tailored tasks and strategies like the Check, Check, Done! checklist can enhance students' ability to effectively manage their learning. These practices not only reinforce the skills taught in direct instruction settings but also empower students to take ownership of their educational journeys, therefore deepening their engagement and understanding.

As we continue to explore the student-engaged framework, the focus will shift to the collaboration station. Here, we will examine strategies and tools to emphasize teamwork and collective problem solving, building on the foundation of independence established in this chapter. By integrating collaborative activities, we aim to enhance communication skills, foster peer relationships, and create a more interactive and cohesive learning environment. This balance of independent and collaborative learning experiences is key to developing well-rounded, engaged students who are prepared to succeed in diverse educational and real-world settings.

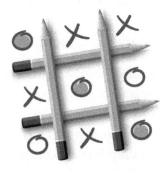

CHAPTER 5
COLLABORATION STATION

The collaboration station in Mrs. O'Donnell's third-grade room is abuzz with student voices as curious minds collaborate to learn about the gold rush while mastering this standard: "Describe the relationship between a series of historical events, scientific ideas or concepts, or steps in technical procedures in a text, using language that pertains to time, sequence, and cause/effect" (RI.3.3; NGA & CCSSO, 2010a).

Five students are at the collaboration station. Among them are Alexis, who has a reading IEP, and Kaelynn, who is in the "gifted and talented program." Here, in this station, labels like "reading IEP" or "gifted and talented program" fade into the background, replaced by the shared purpose of a collaborative project. Anyone who walks into the classroom cannot identify the labels placed on each student.

The group of five decides to break into two smaller groups. In the first group, two students research events that took place during the gold rush to create a chronological Google Slides presentation to share with the class. In the second group, the other three students collaborate to create a timeline infographic highlighting gold rush images and facts. All five students are working toward one common goal of mastering the standard (RI.3.3), while having a choice in how they present the learned information. At the end of the week, the groups share their presentations with the class to showcase their learning.

> *The collaboration station isn't just a snapshot of a lesson; it's a testament to the power of inclusive learning. It's where labels dissolve, replaced by the shared language of inquiry and creation. It's where every student, regardless of their challenges or strengths, finds their place in learning.*

The scenario in Mrs. O'Donnell's third-grade classroom exemplifies the transformative impact of an inclusive and collaborative learning environment. By focusing on a shared goal, students of various abilities and backgrounds come together to engage deeply with the content, demonstrating that effective learning goes beyond traditional labels. This chapter dives into the core principles behind such a dynamic learning station and shows how the collaboration station aligns with educational standards and creates a culture of inclusivity and collaboration.

Throughout this chapter, we explore the foundational elements that make the collaboration station a successful model for engaging students in meaningful learning experiences. We connect these practices to the student-engaged framework, showing how they support the development of essential skills such as critical thinking, communication, and teamwork. Additionally, we outline the strategies for ensuring the station runs smoothly across a typical school week, and provide practical insights for teachers.

By the end of the chapter, readers will gain a comprehensive understanding of how to create and sustain a collaborative learning environment that empowers all students. We discuss the importance of setting clear objectives, modeling how to work collaboratively, and offering flexible presentation options, all of which contribute to a positive classroom environment.

Teacher Self-Awareness Check

To begin your exploration of this topic, use the questions in this section to examine your teaching approach, classroom environments, and student interactions. Through this reflection, honestly observe your own strengths and areas for improvement as you seek to make meaningful changes to enhance student engagement and learning outcomes in your classroom related to student collaboration. (Visit **go.SolutionTree.com/instruction** to access reproducible versions of Teacher Self-Awareness Check sections in this book.)

How often do you have students collaborate? Collaboration does not mean that students are given a checklist and step-by-step directions to complete a task together. True collaboration occurs when students have voice and choice to make decisions within their group and create something the teacher does not clearly define.

Do all students produce the same product when you want to know if they understand a concept or a standard? If so, why?

How might you better empower students to be able to show what they truly know in the format that best showcases their learning?

Understanding the Collaboration Station

The collaboration station serves as a hub for interactive learning experiences, encouraging peer-to-peer engagement, problem solving, and teamwork. The elementary years mark a crucial developmental period during which students acquire fundamental skills and attitudes that shape their future academic and social trajectories. By introducing the collaboration station, educators provide students with opportunities to develop essential life skills such as communication, cooperation, negotiation, and teamwork. Through collaborative tasks and projects, students learn to express their ideas, listen to diverse perspectives, and work collectively toward common goals. These experiences enhance academic learning and lay the groundwork for successful interpersonal relationships in later stages of life.

The collaboration station also emphasizes student agency (the capacity of students to act independently and make their own choices about their learning) through voice and choice as group members determine what they need to do each day to complete their task or project on time. Their communication skills develop as they collaborate, build relationships, and rely on one another to complete their project or task by the final day. Students are all held accountable as they have a deadline for task or project completion.

Choice and differentiation also allow students to explore a specific standard or content area within their preferred assessment format while making decisions with peers and working as a team where they may not always get their first pick. Whereas some students gravitate toward technology, others may prefer hands-on activities where they create a 3-D model, a game board, or a poster. This choice empowers students to engage with the material that best resonates with them. But at this station, students must think of their whole group and not just their individual preferences. While students have options to choose from to show their learning, this station focuses on collaboration. By working together on a shared project, students learn from each other's strengths and perspectives and build relationships with their peers. They learn how to communicate with one another to make collective decisions and become assets to any team on which they serve.

As students learn how to work with peers, manage time, and make collaborative decisions, they incorporate learned skills of communication, accountability, and relationship building with one another. In this way, collaboration stations are an excellent way to promote inclusivity (which benefits both mental well-being and academic success) as students of different backgrounds, experiences, and learning preferences learn to relate to one another. Implemented effectively, these stations ensure students don't feel boxed in and can truly showcase what they know and can do.

This last point is especially important as you consider that students often feel defined by labels the education system foists on them ("low," "gifted," and so on). In our experience, when teachers create a classroom environment that peels away such labels, it can be liberating for students. This requires teachers to shift their views to a presumption of competence for every student within their classroom. According to St. John Fisher University professors and authors Whitney H. Rapp, Katrina L. Arndt, and Susan M. Hildenbrand (2019), our attitudes shape our actions in the classroom. Educators must always assume students are capable until they have evidence otherwise. If we don't presume competence within students, we risk depriving them of learning opportunities that they are capable of succeeding with.

Within the collaboration station, a student is an asset to their group, contributing their strengths and knowledge. The fact that the student has an IEP, for example, is irrelevant to the work of the group, as all students can be successful. The activities at this station should use a STEAM (science, technology, engineering, arts, and mathematics) approach, one that includes inquiry-based, problem-based, project-based, or game-based learning and assessments. We explore each of these applications in the following sections, starting with a focus on problem-based learning and inquiry-based learning, which work together in this context as part of a student-centered teaching approach.

PROBLEM- AND INQUIRY-BASED LEARNING

In this format, students take ownership of their learning because they are the ones driving the inquiry and investigation process, collaborating to solve authentic, real-world problems that lack a single "correct" answer. Rather, students explore multiple solutions to decide which option is best. They brainstorm, research, discuss, and present their findings as a collaborative team, using self-directed learning to research information and problem-solve while developing critical thinking skills.

STEAM activities provide a way to cross content areas, which is authentic to daily life and our students' future jobs. As educational technology expert Sara Wanasek (2024) states, "The goal of STEAM education is to equip students with the ability to approach challenges from various angles, shaping them into flexible learners, capable of applying various skills to novel situations." So, just because you might start with a focus on mathematics, that doesn't mean you can't bring in an authentic learning opportunity from science that connects to or aligns with the mathematics content. For example, while learning about basic addition and subtraction, students could explore the growth of plants. They could plant seeds in different conditions (varied amounts of water or sunlight) and measure the plants' growth over time. To support this activity, students might also create simple charts to record their data and use their mathematics skills to compare the growth rates. Such a hands-on project not only reinforces their understanding of addition and subtraction but also introduces them to scientific concepts like experimentation and data collection, showing them how mathematics and science work together in the real world.

Problem-based learning in a STEAM context is effective because students gain deep firsthand understanding of a topic by engaging with the problem with a growth mindset instead of learning through direct instruction. In the context of group work, they utilize creativity and innovation while improving their communication and collaboration skills as they explore the best solution and why it's best.

This is also where inquiry-based learning comes into play, as students actively question, investigate, and explore their topic, making sense of a wealth of information. An example of a fourth-grade problem-based learning task from a rural Iowa classroom follows.

- **Problem:** A local farm's corn crops are not producing as well as they have in the past. It is a dry summer, even though there was a lot of snow in the previous winter.
- **Student inquiry:** Throughout their learning, students gather questions about agriculture in Iowa. They can capture these on a wonder wall, where students add questions when they have them so everyone can see each other's questions. Their questions may include, What is needed for corn to grow in Iowa? How does the weather impact crop production in a year? and What agricultural items are used in a drought? Of the questions gathered, students will research the ones that interest them to guide their inquiry.
- **Research and investigation:** Students interview a local farmer or invite a specialist to be a virtual guest speaker. They conduct research into what the weather was like, including temperatures, rainfall, and related factors.
- **Solution and presentation:** Based on their research, students present their findings in a poster, a Google Slides presentation, a model, or some other relevant product.

PROJECT-BASED LEARNING

Project-based learning has many of the same components as problem-based learning, such as student-centered and active engagement in authentic learning. The difference is that project-based learning focuses on creating a tangible product or presentation, whereas problem-based learning focuses on solving an open-ended problem or question while the teacher is the facilitator of the learning.

The project-based approach has a more structured framework where the teacher guides students to end with a final project, rather than to find all the answers.

Problem-based learning focuses on developing knowledge and skills required throughout the process of solving a problem and presenting the findings, whereas project-based learning focuses on understanding a certain topic through a tangible presentation.

GAME-BASED COLLABORATION

Game-based collaboration is a type of instructional strategy that incorporates the design of games to achieve teacher-set learning outcomes. It is an innovative teaching method that integrates education and play. It allows students to complete the learning content in a game-based way by creating and collaborating with their peers. Researcher Qi Zhong (2019) states, "Games are the way to learn new things, the way to form and explain knowledge and skills, the way to combine thinking and action, and the important means of children's intellectual development."

Incorporating game-based learning changes the traditional idea of teacher-led instruction to student-centered learning, where students can actively construct their knowledge, learn from one another's strengths, and complete tasks using educational games.

Implementing Collaborative Activities

When we first implemented the student-engaged framework, we thought that the collaboration station would be the easiest to implement because we'd always had students collaborate. We even prided ourselves on making collaboration a big part of our classrooms. We were wrong! In the first week, we realized we'd never had students truly collaborate. Instead, we had been dictating tasks and how students would complete them while pairing students with partners or placing them in small groups. We assigned every aspect of what they did and who they worked with. We ensured everything was laid out and systems were in place so there would be no guesswork on their end. Not only were students not collaborating, but they weren't thinking critically, solving problems, making decisions, effectively communicating, or creating.

During the first week of this station's implementation, arguments and disagreements occurred across student groups, and students got nothing done in their allotted time. They were frustrated with one another and voiced their frustration at home. In parent-teacher conferences, we heard that our students were unhappy—something that had never happened to us. We felt defeated. We soon realized that we needed to adjust and lay a new groundwork to make this a successful, meaningful experience. First, we had to teach and model for students how to collaborate, solve problems, have disagreements, and be creative. We had to take a step back and create a foundation utilizing communication, accountability, and relationships while teaching our students life skills to collaborate successfully.

By the end of our full implementation, conference time had rolled around again, and these conferences were better than ever. Parents talked about how much confidence their children had now and how much they wanted to come to school. Some students even completed unassigned projects at home on the weekend, different projects from the options they chose on their Check, Check, Done! checklists.

Years later, we still have parents say what a pivotal year that was for their children and how it helped shape them into who they became later in life. That is our ultimate goal as teachers. We don't just want our students to be good at school; we want them to be good at life.

In the following sections, we address how to begin collaboration stations by building the foundation (room arrangement and conflict resolution strategies) and then planning out station activities.

BUILD THE FOUNDATION

There is a lot of necessary foundation work to do to help this station succeed, possibly making it the most challenging station to start. Because students work with one another without direct teacher support, you will need a space in the room where students can work collaboratively, which could be desks that are pushed together, a large table, or an area on the floor away from the minilesson, as noisy communication will sometimes happen among the students. Conversation partners must be taught and implemented if they aren't already established (see chapter 1, page 43). Once students know how to have a social conversation, they can apply it to academic and collaborative conversations. Post the conversation chart (figure 1.12, page 44) where students can see it while they are at the collaboration station.

Students also need to know how to disagree without an argument. Conflict is bound to arise when students work together within a classroom, and although conflict can produce several negative consequences, like anger, pain, and sadness, a lot of positive results come from conflict if it is solved constructively. According to David W. Johnson, professor of educational psychology, and Roger T. Johnson (1996), professor of curriculum and instruction at the University of Minnesota:

> Conflicts are constructive when (a) all disputants are satisfied with the outcome (the agreement maximizes joint benefits and allows all participants to achieve their goals and, therefore, everyone goes away satisfied and pleased), (b) the relationship between the disputants is strengthened and improved (disputants are better able to work together and have more respect, trust, and liking for each other), and (c) disputants are able to resolve future conflicts constructively. (p. 2)

To achieve this outcome, we suggest using a disagreement chart, an example of which appears in figure 5.1. This chart provides students with scenarios and options for solving a disagreement through compromise, negotiation, or rock paper scissors.

When we disagree, we can . . .

Disagreement: I want chocolate chip cookies, but Mrs. Helmke wants peanut butter cookies.

Compromise

We could compromise and make chocolate chip peanut butter cookies.

We could compromise and make sugar cookies because we both like sugar cookies.

Negotiation

We could negotiate to make chocolate chip cookies this time and peanut butter cookies next time.

Rock Paper Scissors

We could play rock paper scissors to decide which type of cookies to make. The person who wins two out of three games decides what kind of cookies we make.

FIGURE 5.1: Disagreement chart.

When students understand they have options for solving a disagreement and a time frame, they won't spend the entire station time arguing. If they disagree, you can give them a timer and thirty seconds to solve their disagreement using one of the chart's three options. They must be OK with the outcome; once they have chosen their disagreement strategy, there must be no further arguing about the topic. Other students can also tell their group members to use the chart if they overhear an argument that is not being resolved.

To teach students how to communicate and effectively solve problems and resolve disagreements, you will need to present them with authentic opportunities to practice. One way to do this is to have a board game at the collaboration station when you introduce the station. Students need to learn the rules and then can play the game on their own. As the teacher, when it is time for them to play, take out an important piece of the game, like one of the game pieces or dice. Students will then have to problem-solve about how to move forward in the game. Once they can do this effectively without conflict, you can bring in academic games and projects for students to complete at this station. In this way, they learn how to disagree and utilize the disagreement chart at the station.

PLAN THE STATION ACTIVITY

Once the setting for the collaboration is in place and students are armed with conflict resolution strategies, students are ready to academically participate in the collaboration station. Each week, student groups should be able to show their learning in digital, hands-on, or paper-based ways. You will decide the station's focus and the types of opportunities that are available that week, but students should have voice and choice in completing the projects or tasks.

Look at the standards and content you are covering for the week. What problem-based, project-based, or game-based opportunities can you provide for students to collaborate and showcase their learning? Provide options for students to choose from that will give you what you need in order to see they have learned the necessary standard or content. Use the template in figure 5.2 to help you plan your collaboration.

	Problem-Based Activity	Project-Based Activity	Game-Based Activity	Standard
Paper product				
Digital product				
Model or presentation				

FIGURE 5.2: Collaboration station activity planning template.

Visit go.SolutionTree.com/instruction for a free reproducible version of this figure.

Following are some possible collaboration activity ideas.

- Map with a legend
- Advertisement
- Memoir
- Advice column
- News article
- Job application and résumé
- Biography
- Five things poster
- Persuasive essay
- Brochure
- Script of a play
- Comic strip
- Poem
- Computer game or board game
- Descriptive essay
- Postcards
- Trading cards
- Diary entry
- Invention
- Email conversation
- Recipe
- Diorama
- Restaurant menu
- Model
- Article
- Survival kit
- Historical fiction story
- Song
- How-to essay
- Infographic
- Textbook page
- Informative essay
- Timeline
- Interview
- Letter
- Drop-in to a location
- Twenty questions
- Slides presentation

Once you have a series of standards-aligned activities and end products planned out, it's time to focus on how you'll implement the station. Here, it's much simpler to show than to tell, so let's look at an example collaboration station task and Check, Check, Done! checklist from a third-grade classroom.

For several weeks, students in this class have been learning about the Oregon Trail during social studies, while in literacy, they have been reading informational texts. During mathematics, the students have focused on adding and subtracting with decimals, and in science, they have been exploring motion and design. As a teacher who is planning activities for a collaboration station, think of the opportunities to combine these learning topics instead of teaching each area in isolation. Consider the following interconnections related to this example.

- **Social studies and literacy:** Create a space for students to explore using inquiry. For example, during the 19th century, the Oregon Trail journey involved a lot of planning and decision making for those who undertook the journey. Students can use their informational text–reading skills to research what supplies pioneers needed and the challenges they faced. This research can help them write a plan for their own westward journey, considering factors like food, tools, and weather or any questions about the Oregon Trail they would like to explore.
- **Social studies and mathematics:** Traveling the Oregon Trail involved a lot of measuring and calculating distances. Students can use their decimal addition and subtraction skills to calculate daily travel distances, food consumption rates, and how much fabric they would need to make clothes for the journey as well as budget what money they are allotted through this problem-based activity.
- **Social studies and science:** The Oregon Trail journey was taken by wagon. Students can use their knowledge of motion and design to research and design their own covered wagons. In this project-based learning opportunity, they can consider factors like how to make a wagon strong enough to handle the terrain, light enough to pull, and spacious enough to store supplies when creating models of their wagons.

At the collaboration station, the teacher decided students should have a hands-on opportunity to create a poster of purchases from ads where they must budget, just as pioneers had to budget at each trading post throughout their time on the Oregon Trail. This requires students to add and subtract with decimal points, tying in their mathematics standard. Students could also create a model covered wagon utilizing the science kit pieces from their unit on motion and design.

For a digital activity, the teacher decides to have students create a video comparing and contrasting pioneer life and modern life. (This option also requires digital research.)

To ensure there is an opportunity for writing work (either typed or handwritten), the teacher directs students to create a five-page journal discussing the successes and struggles of life on the Oregon Trail. This activity incorporates elements of inquiry as they determine the successes and struggles.

Finally, the teacher decides to have students take on a teaching mindset in practicing their learning of compound words by putting together a poster or video about their learning.

Figure 5.3 shows an example of a Check, Check, Done! checklist to support the activities not just at the collaboration station but across all the stations for that week's learning.

 Check, Check, Done!

Collaboration Station	
You struck gold! Use the ads to spend $3,000 without going over. Cut out the items you choose, and put them on a poster.	
Create a video comparing and contrasting pioneer life and modern life.	
What successes and struggles did pioneers face on the Oregon Trail? Create five journal entries highlighting them.	
Use the science kit pieces to create a model of a covered wagon.	
Teach compound words to your classmates (using a poster, Google Slides, and so on).	
Independent Work Station	
Complete the graphic organizer.	
Write a rough draft.	
Edit and revise the rough draft.	
Type a final copy.	
Upload the final copy to Seesaw.	

Minilesson Station	
Learn about the standard RI.3.5: I can identify text and graphic features.	
Take an assessment about RI.3.5.	
Learn about compound words.	
Learn about the social studies lesson on the Oregon Trail.	
Digital Content Station	
Read and watch videos about the Oregon Trail on Epic! (class code: abcde).	
# Video: Compound words	
# Video: Pioneer life and the gold rush	
Play *The Oregon Trail*.	

Question From Your Research

_____

_____

_____

_____

Source for standard: NGA & CCSSO, 2010a.

FIGURE 5.3: Oregon Trail Check, Check, Done! checklist.

*Visit **go.SolutionTree.com/instruction** for a free reproducible version of this figure.*

Conclusion

The collaboration station is an important component of the student-engaged framework, serving as a dynamic space where students can work together, share ideas, and develop essential communication and teamwork skills. This chapter highlighted the importance of fostering a collaborative classroom environment where students learn to value diverse perspectives and contribute to collective problem-solving efforts. By integrating collaboration into daily activities, we prepare students for the interconnected world they will encounter beyond the classroom.

Looking ahead to the next chapter, we will explore the digital content station, where students will have the opportunity to work both independently and collaboratively using various digital tools. This transition builds on the principles of the collaboration station, demonstrating how technology can further enhance student engagement and learning. In the digital content station, students will continue to develop their ability to navigate different learning pathways, adapt to new challenges, and collaborate effectively, all within a technology-rich environment.

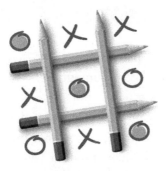

CHAPTER 6
DIGITAL CONTENT STATION

In Ms. Johnson's vibrant and tech-infused classroom, the digital content station is humming with excited chatter and the soft clicks of keyboards as students engage in a carefully crafted blend of independent learning and collaborative work. Students use their devices to access educational websites tailored to their individual learning levels. Some are engrossed in interactive grammar lessons, while others explore digital books that align with their reading abilities and the content they are learning as a whole group. Ms. Johnson has curated a list of websites that allow students to independently work at their own pace, that provide data for her to use to guide instruction, and that engage students in the content.

Other students are divided into small groups to conduct research related to their current unit of study. They use online resources to gather information, collaborate on Google Docs, and create multimedia presentations with tools like Canva or Adobe Express. As the students choose their learning path within the digital content station for the day, a harmonious blend of independence and collaboration emerges. The technology seamlessly integrates into the learning process, allowing students to absorb information and actively collaborate, create, problem-solve, and communicate.

When the timer signals the end of the digital content station, students excitedly share their learning on the online learning platforms, talk about the levels they progressed through, and discuss the next steps for their research projects while

> lining up. The atmosphere is one of accomplishment and camaraderie, showcasing successful integration of technology into the classroom and preparing students for the world outside of school.

As we transition from the lively scene in Ms. Johnson's classroom to a broader discussion on the role of digital content stations in educational settings, it is important to recognize how much stations embody the principles of modern educational technology. This chapter, focusing on digital content stations, aims to give teachers a structured understanding of how they can integrate technology in a way that enhances learning while maintaining a balance between independence and collaboration among students.

A digital content station, like the one in Ms. Johnson's classroom, is just a small version of the school's broader educational technology framework. The digital content station is not about isolated tools; it is an integral component of a comprehensive educational strategy. It helps create a blend of individualized learning and cooperative engagement, which is important in developing skills necessary for the digital age. In this chapter, we explore the setup, management, and use of the digital content station. We discuss how this station can be tailored to accommodate diverse learning styles and levels and how it can be used to track student progress through data-driven insights. This allows for targeted instruction and continuous adjustment of learning paths, which are crucial for effective teaching and learning.

By the end of this final chapter, you should understand how you can effectively integrate digital content stations into daily classroom activities and how these stations align with overall educational objectives. Our goal is to equip teachers with the knowledge and tools to implement these stations in a way that maximizes student engagement and educational outcomes, preparing students for both academic success and future digital competencies.

Teacher Self-Awareness Check

To begin your exploration of this topic, use the questions in this section to examine your teaching approach, classroom environments, and student interactions. Through this reflection, honestly observe your own strengths and areas for improvement as you seek to make meaningful changes to enhance student engagement and learning outcomes in your classroom related to the use of technology. (Visit **go.SolutionTree.com/instruction** to access reproducible versions of Teacher Self-Awareness Check sections in this book.)

Do you have students use technology, and if so, how often?

Do you have students use their devices to work only independently, work only collaboratively, or do a combination of both?

Is what you are asking students to do designed with a purpose? If so, what specific skills does it target?

Are students working on websites targeting specific skills you've taught them?

Will the websites they use provide you with student data? What data will you collect?

```
_____
_____
_____
_____
```

Do your students know why they are getting on specific websites?

```
_____
_____
_____
_____
```

Understanding the Digital Content Station

The education system has significantly transformed in the years following the COVID-19 pandemic and continues to evolve rapidly. In his analysis of COVID-19 distance learning, Hattie (2021) highlights evidence suggesting a significant potential enhancement in teaching methodologies and student learning outcomes with technology. He urges educators to integrate a wider array of digital tools in the classroom to enrich learning experiences. This shift presents an opportunity for educators to harness technology's capabilities in creating more dynamic learning environments that expand beyond traditional, one-size-fits-all teaching methods.

The use of technology is an integral part of education and has revolutionized the way students learn. In their book *Infusing Technology in the K–5 Classroom*, Valerie Morrison, Stephanie Novak, and Tim Vanderwerff (2019) state:

> Today's students come to school knowing more technology than ever before. New educational research suggests that offering a variety of learning opportunities, including technology options, may be the best way to engage today's generation of learners. Educators must respond to this generation and address its unique learning needs. (p. 21)

Integrating technology in the classroom is about more than just teaching basic computer skills; it's about effectively using technology to deepen and enhance the learning process. To further this goal, the digital content station gives students access to digital tools to enhance their learning. It is a designated area in the classroom where students can use a wide range of digital content, such as educational videos, interactive games, and online resources. According to Morrison and colleagues (2019):

> This generation of students needs to be engaged in active and interactive learning to enhance their knowledge. They do not want technology just because it is "cool." They need technology because it drives their world (now and in the future). They are looking for something dynamic to make learning come alive—to make it different and interesting every day. Being connected accomplishes that goal. (p. 24)

The digital content station provides a time and place for students to engage in and explore new concepts in a fun and interactive way on their own and with others. Across the following sections, we examine several benefits of integrating digital content into our student-engaged framework, including not just pure engagement but also creativity and personalized learning.

ENGAGEMENT

Traditional teaching methods can fail students in terms of motivation and engagement because worksheets and tests don't allow students to connect to their learning. In an International Society for Technology in Education (ISTE) blog post, technology coordinator Nicholas Provenzano (2023) explains how learning during the pandemic showed that teacher-led instruction and rote memorization were not the best ways to engage students. Many schools shifted toward activities and pacing directed by the students. Research from Avneet Hira and Emma Anderson (2021) shows that this shift meant educators could offer various technology to support learning and help students actively engage while gaining knowledge and skills. With students and teachers back in classrooms, it is important not to fall back into old habits that don't promote students' active participation in their learning. Getting the most out of technology means providing students with a wide variety of learning approaches and modalities to help them succeed and fully engage in class.

By incorporating digital tools and resources into the learning process, teachers can tap into students' natural curiosity and use it to their advantage. Digital content, such as educational games and videos, can make learning more exciting and enjoyable for students and lead to deeper understanding of the subject matter.

For example, students can use digital whiteboards to solve mathematics problems, do drag-and-drop activities to learn new vocabulary, and play educational games to reinforce concepts.

In her book *Eight Myths of Student Disengagement*, Jennifer A. Fredricks (2014) says many students are just going through the motions and are not emotionally and cognitively engaged, meaning they will not develop the higher-order and critical thinking skills necessary to compete for future jobs. Research from Hao Lei, Yunhuo Cui, and Wenye Zhou (2018) shows that student engagement is a strong predictor of achievement-related outcomes, meaning students with higher engagement have higher grades and score better on standardized tests.

As educators, we want to both teach our students and inspire them with engaging activities that we weave into their daily learning experiences. A significant benefit of having a digital content station is that it increases student engagement and motivation. In *Disruptive Thinking in Our Classrooms*, Sheninger (2021) concludes, "The old drill-and-kill method is neurologically useless, as it turns out. Relevant, meaningful activities that both engage students emotionally and connect with what they already know are what help build neural connections and long-term memory storage" (p. 59). Interactive activities require students to actively participate in their learning; therefore, these activities help students cognitively engage with the content and retain it.

REAL-WORLD LEARNING AND CREATIVITY

In a technology-driven world, the digital content station provides access to a vast array of educational resources beyond traditional textbooks. Students can explore virtual simulations, drop into different locations, explore content using online encyclopedias and educational websites, and expand their knowledge and foster research skills. Technology also offers a gateway to global information and perspectives that allows students to explore diverse cultures and global issues, connect with students around the world, and gain a broader understanding of the world outside the four walls of the classroom.

Further, when teachers combine creativity with technology use, they see even better outcomes. According to ISTE blogger and journalist Nicole Krueger (2022), "Teachers who frequently assign classwork involving creativity are more likely to observe higher-order cognitive skills—problem solving, critical thinking, [and] making connections between subjects—in their students." As Lesley University (n.d.) reports, these skills, which are well represented in a STEAM curriculum, are vital for learners as they prepare for life after school: "The U.S. Bureau of Labor Statistics forecasts there will be almost 11 million job openings in STEM-related fields by 2029." Incorporating the components of STEAM into the digital content station allows students to begin solving problems and thinking critically and provides students with tools and methods for discovering new and inventive ways to learn.

Students can express their creativity through multimedia projects, digital art, and other innovative activities. Exposure to various resources enhances their creative skills, develops their critical thinking skills, and encourages them to become lifelong learners (Krueger, 2022).

PERSONALIZATION

As we discussed previously in this book, every student has unique learning preferences, and meeting these individual needs is essential to ensure their academic success. With the digital content station, teachers can personalize each student's learning experience through the lens of UDL, which guides educational practice by providing flexibility in how information is presented and how students engage in the content (CAST, 2018). For example, a student who is a visual learner might watch educational videos and look at images and charts that can help them better understand concepts. At the same time, a student who is an auditory learner might listen to recordings or podcasts on the concepts.

Using digital tools, students with different learning abilities and needs can participate in the learning process without feeling left out. This inclusivity creates a more equitable learning environment, where every student has an equal opportunity to learn and succeed. Sheninger (2021) explains that technology allows for personalized learning opportunities, culminating in a shift from consumption to creation and curation, which engages students in their learning experiences. For example, a student who struggles with traditional reading can use text-to-speech software to better understand the material, while another student might use digital storytelling tools to create a multimedia presentation; both students engage with the content in ways that suit their individual learning styles.

Implementing Digital Activities

When implementing the digital content station, teachers must understand the purpose behind their technology selections so that these selections are deliberate in optimizing learning outcomes. Rather than allowing devices, tools, or websites to dictate instruction, educators should focus on the rationale behind the technology they incorporate. The main objective of incorporating technology is to offer students enhanced opportunities for learning and critical thinking. Increasing engagement is important, but teachers must also consider how digital tools can enrich learning experiences and provide clarity and relevance for students.

For example, when choosing a digital tool for a mathematics lesson, a teacher might select an interactive app that lets students manipulate shapes to better understand geometric concepts. This choice is deliberate and aligns with the learning objectives of enhancing spatial reasoning skills.

Sheninger (2021) discusses how tying a relevant lesson or activity to a digital tool empowers students to use their knowledge to construct an understanding of the course material. Learning becomes more durable and lasting when students are cognitively engaged in the learning process. Long-term retention, understanding, and transfer result from mental work on the part of learners engaged in active sense making and knowledge construction. To achieve this, teachers should do the following.

1. **Identify learning objectives:** Clearly define what students should know and be able to do after the lesson.
2. **Select appropriate tools:** Choose digital tools that directly support these learning objectives and provide opportunities for critical thinking and creativity.
3. **Integrate tools thoughtfully:** Ensure that the use of technology is seamlessly integrated into the lesson plan so it enhances rather than distracts from the learning experience.
4. **Provide guidance and support:** Offer students clear instructions and support on how to use the technology effectively. This could be a quick minilesson where the students come back to meet with the teacher.
5. **Assess and reflect:** Continuously assess the technology's effectiveness in meeting learning objectives, and be willing to make adjustments as needed.

When planning for the week, make sure you have a mixture of independent and collaborative activities for students to complete at the digital content station. Having a mixture of activities related to the content they are learning can enhance the students' experiences within the classroom. A planning document, like the one depicted in figure 6.1, can help you plan your digital content station.

Standard or Content	Independent Activities	Collaborative Activities
3.OA.A.1: Interpret products of whole numbers, e.g., interpret 5 × 7 as the total number of objects in 5 groups of 7 objects each.	Do the assigned standard work on Freckle.	Connect Four: Multiplying by multiples

	Complete the Seesaw multiplication activity.	Multiplication tic-tac-toe
	Play the SplashLearn game.	
	Watch the video of the "Multiplication Mash-Up" song. Then, complete the Quizizz assignment.	

Source for standard: NGA & CCSSO, 2010b.

FIGURE 6.1: Example digital content station planning document.

*Visit **go.SolutionTree.com/instruction** for a free reproducible version of this figure.*

The following sections take a closer look at the differences between implementing independent and collaborative digital content stations.

INDEPENDENT IMPLEMENTATION

Leveraging the digital content station and technology empowers students to independently learn with tools and resources that cater to their individual learning styles and paces. There are a wide variety of activities and platforms you can tap into to enhance student engagement and learning regardless of your curriculum. Let's look at some examples. After each example, you will find a brief description of the tool or website.

- **Educational games:** Many websites and apps make learning fun by turning review sessions into interactive games, promoting active participation and reinforcing knowledge. While there are other excellent options that could be listed here, the following are some options for you to consider.
    + *Kahoot! (https://kahoot.com)*—A game-based learning platform
    + *Quizizz (https://quizizz.com)*—A learning platform that offers multiple tools to make a classroom fun, interactive, and engaging
    + *Seesaw (https://seesaw.com)*—A student-driven digital portfolio with online activities created and ready to use

- *Quizlet (https://quizlet.com)*—A website that creates study sets and flash cards
- *Blooket (https://blooket.com)*—A website that offers a unique take on trivia and review games
- *Boddle (https://boddlelearning.com)*—A website that makes mathematics engaging for learners
- *Freckle (https://freckle.com)*—A student-centered and teacher-driven program for all instructional areas (Freckle adapts at the "just-right" level, with student-friendly incentives and age-appropriate designs to provide a balance of fun and learning.)

These programs not only support and facilitate student learning but also offer immediate data for teachers to use. These data inform teachers about students' progress on a standard, giving them appropriate information to make instructional decisions.

- **Coding and programming:** Online coding programs teach students the basics of coding through engaging project-based activities, helping them develop critical thinking skills and problem-solving skills. Teachers will often have coding as an option for students to pick from throughout the week because students can highly engage and work on their problem-solving skills by breaking down problems, analyzing them, putting solutions together, and solving challenges creatively. Coding programs such as the following are easy to use for beginners.
  - *Code.org (https://code.org)*—Coding and computer science education
  - *Kodable (https://kodable.com)*—Programming for K–5 students
  - *Tynker (https://tynker.com)*—Coding and game development for all school levels
  - *Scratch (https://scratch.mit.edu)*—A block-based coding platform

- **Digital storytelling:** Programs like the following allow students to create and share their own stories, encouraging creativity and improving their writing and communication abilities.
  - *Book Creator (https://bookcreator.com)*—A tool for creating interactive digital books
  - *Google Slides (https://workspace.google.com/products/slides)*—A presentation creation tool
  - *Prezi (https://prezi.com)*—A presentation creation tool

- **Collaborative projects:** Tools like the following allow students to collaborate on documents, presentations, and summary handouts, fostering teamwork and communication skills.
    + *Google Slides (https://workspace.google.com/products/slides)*—A presentation creation tool
    + *Adobe Express (https://adobe.com/express)*—A collection of software tools for creating graphics, videos, animations, and so on (formerly known as Adobe Spark)
    + *Canva (https://canva.com)*—An online tool that allows you to create slideshows, book reviews, pamphlets, and graphic organizers that capture the group's thinking

- **Digital portfolios:** A number of tools empower students to independently collect and showcase their work to demonstrate progress, which promotes ownership of their learning and builds self-confidence. Many of the preceding online platforms can be used for this purpose, such as Seesaw, Google Slides, and Canva. For example, a fourth-grade mathematics standards portfolio might enable students to display their understanding of the standards and their learning progression for the standards throughout the year. The portfolio could include samples of the student's work, reflections on their learning process, and self-assessments that demonstrate their mastery of a specific standard.

    A digital portfolio not only supports teachers in assessing a student's proficiency with learning standards but also provides a real-time way to communicate with parents or guardians about their child's progress. By viewing the portfolio, parents can see concrete examples of their child's work and development, creating better school-home connections and providing insights that help support their child's learning journey.

Independent use of technology is a powerful tool, offering a diverse and engaging landscape for students' independent exploration and knowledge acquisition. But for digital content stations to be effective, teachers must demonstrate how to navigate the chosen technology, highlighting appropriate usage and safety protocols. Provide clear instruction and remind students to use Brain, Buddy, Buddy if they are not sure how to use a certain website or tool (see page 33). Once modeling and scaffolding have taken place, it is important to gradually release responsibility to students as they independently explore their learning via digital content stations. Students can then explore concepts and content at their own pace to become self-directed learners.

The digital content station further allows teachers to cater to students' individual needs and learning preferences. Imagine students diving into an interactive game to refine their reading skills, support them through struggles with mathematical concepts, visualize geometric concepts through animation programs, or express their creativity through multimedia presentations. The McREL International study *Student Engagement: Evidence-Based Strategies to Boost Academic and Social-Emotional Results* (Abla & Fraumeni, 2019) explains that a teacher can indeed get better results if they have technology tools available.

COLLABORATIVE IMPLEMENTATION

Collaboration within the digital content station is a crucial skill for students to develop, as it allows them to work together, share ideas, and enhance their learning through various digital tools. Students can cocreate presentations utilizing platforms like Google Slides, while Seesaw allows them to give feedback on their peers' work and receive feedback on their own. Tools like Quizizz and Kahoot! encourage group participation and collective problem solving, creating a sense of teamwork and collaborative effort. By collaboratively engaging with digital content, students not only deepen their understanding of the subject matter but also build essential skills in communication, cooperation, and digital literacy. Fredricks (2014) states:

> The focus on isolated student work stems in part from our assessment-driven educational system in which academic preparation for standardized tests has become the priority. In this context, many teachers feel that addressing the social dimensions of the classroom and developing a sense of community are less essential aspects of their roles and instructional time. This narrowing focus on academic content without peer interaction has made it difficult for some students to develop the social skills necessary to be successful today and may be contributing to the sense of isolation and alienation that many students feel. (p. 162)

Technology enhances collaboration by connecting students with peers to work together on projects, share ideas, communicate, and provide feedback effectively. For example, if students are learning about the American Revolution, collaborative groups of students can read books on the children's book platform Epic! (https://getepic.com), conduct research using student-friendly search engines like TrueFlix (https://scholastic.com/digital/trueflix), or read books pulled from the school library. Providing access to and choice across a vast collection of ebooks, audiobooks, and physical books gives students diverse ways to effectively engage with content and collaborate.

Students take notes as directed by the teacher, ensuring they include all the necessary information. Afterward, student groups create a digital slideshow or other product that includes their notes, images, embedded videos, and so on to represent their learning progress. Students can prioritize what each group member will be in charge of within the assignment, giving everyone an equal opportunity to contribute and learn from one another. When done, students share their presentations with the whole class and teacher and highlight their research and collaborative, speaking, and listening skills. Through this process, students engage in collaboration, verbal communication, creativity, and problem solving, which are all areas psychologist and career consultant Natalia Peart (2019) emphasizes as some of the most important skills needed in the workforce outside of school.

Before having students collaborate with technology, you must set clear expectations and guidelines for collaboration in the classroom. As Fredricks (2014) explains, encouraging students to talk to each other about assignments, work in small groups, and move around the classroom as they do activities leads to more positive social outcomes and peer relations. So, teach students about digital etiquette, responsible use, and respect of others' ideas and contributions. Begin by having students explain what collaboration using technology would look, sound, and feel like when done appropriately. Once rules are established, it is important to then integrate regular feedback and reflection sessions into the collaborative activities. Encourage students to assess their teamwork and problem-solving skills and the effectiveness of the technology tool they used in order to promote continuous improvement and overall development of the students' ability to work with peers.

Conclusion

The digital content station serves as the capstone of the student-engaged framework, seamlessly integrating technology to enhance both independent and collaborative learning experiences. In this station, students leverage digital tools to explore content, conduct research, create projects, and engage with peers, thereby developing critical skills that are essential for success in the modern world. The digital content station not only supports personalized learning paths but also facilitates innovative collaboration, where students connect and work together in new and exciting ways.

By incorporating the digital content station into the student-engaged framework, we provide students with versatile and adaptive learning environments that mirror the complexities and demands of the real world. This approach empowers students to take ownership of their learning, encourages creativity, and prepares them to navigate the ever-evolving digital landscape. As we conclude our exploration of the student-engaged framework, it is clear that the integration of digital tools, collaborative strategies, and personalized learning opportunities creates a robust and dynamic educational experience that develops well-rounded, technology-proficient, and engaged learners.

This chapter brings to a close part 2 of this book and its focus on the four learning stations that make up the student-engaged framework. As you start to implement these stations, use the Check, Check, Done! checklist shown in figure 6.2 to help guide you through this work.

Check, Check, Done!
Planning Your Stations

Planning the Minilesson Station	
Determine what standards you will focus on for the week.	
Decide what types of groupings you will use—homogeneous, heterogeneous, or random.	
Decide what assessments and resources you will use with your students. Will they all be the same or different?	
Planning the Independent Work Station	
Identify focus standards, define what proficiency of each standard looks like, and provide exemplary work examples for students.	
Have students set small goals and identify action steps.	
Plan a variety of relevant learning tasks.	
Collect prioritized student work and provide feedback.	
Collaborate with support staff to personalize activities.	
Planning the Collaboration Station	
Make a "Tools We Know How to Use" list for students to access.	
Decide which activities or ideas you will utilize for the week.	
Teach students how to disagree, and provide them with conflict resolution tools.	
Set up a space in the room where students can work together.	
Determine what skill you would like students to learn during the week, such as decision making, time management, and so on.	

Planning the Digital Content Station	
Determine the instructional strategy or standard you are teaching, and pair it with a tool that will enhance the learning.	
Use the "Digital Content Station Planning Document" (figure 6.1, page 130) to help guide your digital content station.	
List the tech tools your students know how to use and which ones you want them to learn in the "Digital Content Tech Tool Planning Template" (figure 6.3).	

FIGURE 6.2: Check, Check, Done! checklist for planning stations.

*Visit **go.SolutionTree.com/instruction** for a free reproducible version of this figure.*

Introduce one station at a time, or plan and implement all stations within a week. For the digital content station, we suggest using the planning template shown in figure 6.3. This tool will help you organize and plan the digital content station to make it easier to implement technology-infused activities.

Technology Tool Students Will Use	How and When It Will Be Used	Tool Modeled and Taught (Put a check mark here when completed.)

FIGURE 6.3: Digital content tech tool planning template.

*Visit **go.SolutionTree.com/instruction** for a free reproducible version of this figure.*

Epilogue

The student-engaged framework offers a comprehensive blueprint for transforming your classroom's educational practices and cultivating a positive and inclusive learning environment where students are no longer recipients of knowledge but active participants in their own education. By embracing the student-engaged framework, educators can foster a culture of empowerment, engagement, and excitement among learners, igniting their curiosity and passion for learning.

Students are equipped with the tools necessary to thrive in an ever-evolving world through the intentional integration of skills such as critical thinking, creativity, communication, and collaboration. As you embark on this journey, remain committed to the belief that every student has the potential to achieve greatness when provided with opportunities and support to grow. You can inspire the next generation of lifelong learners and future leaders with the student-engaged framework.

When starting with the student-engaged framework, you may begin with one station and introduce additional stations gradually, at whatever pace works for you and your students. For those who prefer a more clearly laid-out plan, we have included an appendix (page 141) with an implementation guide, two practice units, and a blank Check, Check, Done! checklist template to support your efforts.

Whatever journey or path you choose when implementing the student-engaged framework, know it is a process worth providing your students. Soon, you will see more independence, effective workers, higher engagement, and interdependent learners effectively owning their learning.

Appendix

This appendix includes the following resources to support implementation of the student-engaged framework.

- An implementation guide that walks you through a four-week plan
- Two practice units: (1) a penguin unit tailored to kindergarten through second grade and (2) a solar system unit for third grade through fifth grade (Use these to practice procedures and build independence within your students before implementing more rigorous academic content into the stations.)
- A blank reproducible "Check, Check, Done! Checklist Template" (page 153)

Implementation Guide

This implementation guide is organized as a four-week plan, starting with a week of teaching students the foundational pieces of the student-engaged framework while introducing one station from the framework at a time. Beginning in week two, students start to independently practice two stations a day while the teacher facilitates learning. Weeks three and four are flexible; they depend on how your students respond and how effectively they execute the learning stations. Start with three stations a day and shift to four so full implementation occurs during week four.

Although this example is laid out in four weeks, you may choose to reorganize and complete it with your students in a shorter or longer amount of time, depending on your needs and those of your students. For example, students in grades K–2 may need more time to become familiar with the norms you establish around each station. Every school and classroom environment is different, so this is just one option for implementation you might consider. Use what you learn from this book and your firsthand experiences and knowledge to adjust as needed to fit your classroom's needs.

Figure A.1 lays out when to introduce each station and how many stations students will work on each week. Figures A.2 and A.3 (page 144) organize and explain topics that you can address during weeks one and two of implementation. Finally, figures A.4 (page 145) and A.5 (page 146) are templates for adding grade-level content to learning stations. You can also use the Check, Check, Done! checklists you've seen throughout this book, the later unit examples in this appendix, and the blank reproducible version of the checklist (page 153) during these later weeks to introduce students to learning stations.

Week	Monday	Tuesday	Wednesday	Thursday	Friday
One	Foundation week: Whole-group learning to be continued weeklong	Whole-group learning and independent work station	Whole-group learning and digital content station	Whole-group learning and collaboration station	Whole-group learning and minilesson station
Two	Whole-group learning	Two stations: Minilesson and independent work	Two stations: Minilesson and digital content	Two stations: Minilesson and collaboration	Three stations: Minilesson, independent work, and digital content
Three	Whole-group learning	Three stations: Digital content, independent work, and collaboration	Repetition of three stations (digital content, independent work, and collaboration), or all four stations	Four stations	Four stations
Four	Whole-group learning with four stations	Whole-group learning with four stations	Whole-group learning with four stations	Whole-group learning with four stations	Whole-group learning with four stations

FIGURE A.1: Four-week implementation outline.

*Visit **go.SolutionTree.com/instruction** for a free reproducible version of this figure.*

Teach the Whole Group

Soft Start

- Set up expectations for each station and how students will rotate throughout the week.

Conversation Partners

- Set up partners (match strong communicators with those who need practice).
- Teach expectations of partners (location, eye contact, and so on).
- Go through the conversation partner anchor chart (figure 1.12, page 44).
- Practice!

Brain, Buddy, Buddy

- Set up Brain, Buddy, Buddy groups and have them posted.
- Teach how to check with yourself first and then seek help.

Disagreement Chart

- Teach how to have a disagreement and be OK with the outcome.
- Post the disagreement chart (figure 5.1, page 117) around the room at locations near the collaboration station and the digital content station.
- Practice!

Check, Check, Done!

- Put the station activities and standards students will be learning in a Check, Check, Done! checklist.
- Have students check off a task when they complete it.

Stations

- Set up your room so the stations are clearly designated.
- Create a visual for students to use when going through stations.
- Have your students go through the stations and change how much time they will be at each station. They should rotate and be at the next stations within one minute, spending one to three minutes total at each station. This allows students time to practice transitions.

FIGURE A.2: Week one implementation guide (foundation week).

*Visit **go.SolutionTree.com/instruction** for a free reproducible version of this figure.*

Minilesson Station

- Teach expectations for working in a small group with the teacher.
- Check to make sure students have all their necessary items: assistive devices, pencils, and any other items you determine they need during the minilesson.
- Have students practice by working together to listen to a story and complete a graphic organizer based on a specific standard.

Independent Work Station

- Teach expectations: appropriate voice level, what to do when unsure ("Brain, Buddy, Buddy"), what engagement with activities should look like, and so on.
- Have students practice what productive learning at this station looks like by giving them an independent activity to complete.

Collaboration Station

- Teach expectations: appropriate voice level (especially important for group work), what it looks like to work with peers, when to use technology, and so on.
- Teach students how to play selected board games and the importance of honest gameplay in game-based collaboration. If there is a disagreement, practice using the disagreement chart.

Digital Content Station

- Teach expectations: appropriate voice level, proper use of technology at the station, where students go online when they get to this station, and so on.
- Provide headphones if students are watching a video or accessing sites with music or other audio.
- Have a backup plan for when a site doesn't work so students know what to do.
- Model how to lose and how to win.

FIGURE A.3: Week two implementation guide.

*Visit **go.SolutionTree.com/instruction** for a free reproducible version of this figure.*

> **Directions:** Add your specific grade-level content to learning stations. During week three of implementation, you will want to revisit expectations at each station. Assign an activity at each station that students can do to show they understand and can follow expectations.

Minilesson Station

Ensure students know the following expectations.

- I will come prepared to the minilesson station with my Check, Check, Done! checklist, pencil, and notebook.
- I will work for the full station time and do my personal best.
- I will be respectful of others' thoughts and opinions.

Independent Work Station

Ensure students know the following expectations.

- I will work independently.
- If I don't know, I will use Brain, Buddy, Buddy.
- I will work for the full station time and do my personal best.

Determine the activity. The assigned activity should be something that every student can complete on their own. It could be of various levels, based on where the students need to independently practice. This station should not be used for new content. For example, you might have students match compound words and draw a picture of the meaning of a compound word, including a definition and a sentence using the compound word.

Collaboration Station

Ensure students know the following expectations.

- When I have a disagreement, I will use the disagreement chart.
- I will use a level 1 or level 2 voice when talking with my group members.
- I will do my personal best the entire time.

Determine the activity. For example, you might provide students with a familiar game and take out one of the game pieces. Let the students know there is a challenge they will have to solve while playing the game. Also, let them know they most likely will not finish the game that day, so they will need to work together to figure out a way to document where they are so they can continue the game the following day.

Digital Content Station

Ensure students know the following expectations.

- I will work collaboratively with a partner, sharing one screen.
- I will use assigned sites to complete my work.
- I will use my level 1 whisper voice.
- If I don't know, I will use Brain, Buddy, Buddy.

Determine the activity.

FIGURE A.4: Week three implementation guide.

*Visit **go.SolutionTree.com/instruction** for a free reproducible version of this figure.*

Directions: Add your specific grade-level content to learning stations. Starting week three of stations, students should have a good understanding of expectations at each station. This week, you can add content standards, and students can begin to dive into academics at all stations.

Minilesson Station

This week, students will be guided through practice and implementation of standard _____ _____. Students will be introduced to the standard, practice with the group, and be formatively and independently assessed.

Independent Work Station

This week, students will practice standard _____ by _____. Students should _____.

Collaboration Station

Students will work together to create one of the following (of their choosing).

- Product 1: _____
- Product 2: _____
- Product 3: _____
- Product 4: _____

The product students choose to create should convey an understanding of _____ _____ as well as the following traits: _____.

Digital Content Station

Students will _____ using the following digital resources: _____. With their partner or group, they should convey an understanding of _____ as well as the following traits: _____.

FIGURE A.5: Week four implementation guide.

*Visit **go.SolutionTree.com/instruction** for a free reproducible version of this figure.*

Practice Unit for Kindergarten Through Second Grade

This section offers a one-week unit on penguins that is tailored to kindergartners through second graders. You can use this unit to practice procedures and build your students' independence or to deepen your knowledge of how to implement the student-engaged framework in ways that specifically align to your curriculum. This example unit is designed around a high-interest topic, is not aligned with standards, and teaches students about the different learning stations in a low-risk academic setting.

During the unit, focus on building interpersonal and executive functioning skills within your students. Take time to practice routines, thoroughly explain the stations, and implement the visuals and tools that accompany them so students are completely familiar with the learning environment and can navigate it independently. Feel free to use the Check, Check, Done! checklist in figure A.6 as is or create your own using the blank reproducible "Check, Check, Done! Checklist Template" (page 153). Figure A.7 (page 149) and figure A.8 (page 150) each represent a tool that the Check, Check, Done! checklist tasks students with completing.

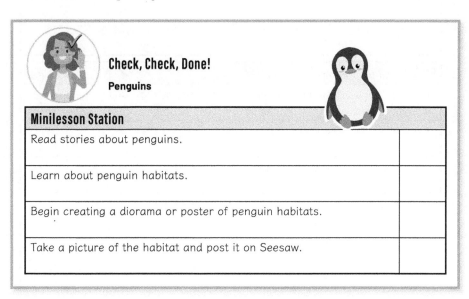

FIGURE A.6: Grades K–2 penguin Check, Check, Done! checklist.

continued ▶

Independent Work Station
Listen to a story about penguins on Epic!
Make a penguin using different craft materials—construction paper, googly eyes, and so on.
Write a short story about your penguin going on an adventure.
Practice reading into Seesaw. Read three times before you start recording! |–
Collaboration Station
Research a penguin on PebbleGo.
Write down five facts about your penguin on your fact sheet.
Create a poster to share with the class.
Digital Content Station
Take a virtual tour of a penguin exhibit, and write or draw about what you learned.
Watch the "How to Draw a Penguin" video.
Write a sentence about the penguin you drew from the video.
Watch the read-aloud video for the book *If You Were a Penguin*.
Fill out the *If You Were a Penguin* worksheet.

*Visit **go.SolutionTree.com/instruction** for a free reproducible version of this figure.*

All About _____ Penguins

Body	Habitat

Food	Family

Interesting Facts

FIGURE A.7: Penguin fact sheet.

*Visit **go.SolutionTree.com/instruction** for a free reproducible version of this figure.*

If You Were a Penguin

By Wendell and Florence Minor

Draw a penguin inside the box.

If I were a penguin, I would . . .

_____

_____

_____

_____

_____

FIGURE A.8: *If You Were a Penguin* worksheet.

Visit **go.SolutionTree.com/instruction** *for a free reproducible version of this figure.*

Appendix

Practice Unit for Third Grade Through Fifth Grade

This section offers a one-week unit on the solar system that is tailored to third graders through fifth graders. You can use this unit to practice procedures and build your students' independence or to deepen your knowledge of how to implement the student-engaged framework in ways that specifically align to your curriculum. This example unit is designed around a high-interest topic, is not aligned with standards, and teaches students about the different learning stations in a low-risk academic setting.

During the unit, focus on building your students' interpersonal and executive functioning skills. Take time to practice routines, thoroughly explain the stations, and implement the visuals and tools that accompany them so students are completely familiar with the learning environment and can navigate it independently. Feel free to use the Check, Check, Done! checklist in figure A.9 as is or create your own using the blank reproducible "Check, Check, Done! Checklist Template" (page 153).

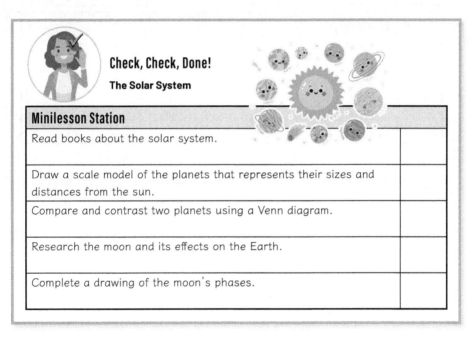

Check, Check, Done!
The Solar System

Minilesson Station	
Read books about the solar system.	
Draw a scale model of the planets that represents their sizes and distances from the sun.	
Compare and contrast two planets using a Venn diagram.	
Research the moon and its effects on the Earth.	
Complete a drawing of the moon's phases.	

FIGURE A.9: Grades 3–5 solar system Check, Check, Done! checklist.

continued ▶

Independent Work Station
Read books about the planets on Epic!
Make a planet using different craft materials—construction paper, glue, and so on.
Write a short story about going on an adventure to another planet.
Practice reading into Seesaw. Read three times before you start recording!

Collaboration Station
Research a planet on PebbleGo.
Write down five to ten facts about your planet on your fact sheet.
Create a poster to share with the class.

Digital Content Station
Watch videos on the solar system that your teacher has bookmarked for you.
Take a virtual tour of the solar system (for example, https://tinyurl.com/34sfxekk).
Visit the NASA Space Place website (https://spaceplace.nasa.gov) to explore the Earth and space.

Visit **go.SolutionTree.com/instruction** *for a free reproducible version of this figure.*

Check, Check, Done! Checklist Template

Lesson or Unit: _____

Minilesson Station	

Independent Work Station	

Collaboration Station	

Digital Content Station	

References and Resources

Abla, C., & Fraumeni, B. R. (2019). *Student engagement: Evidence-based strategies to boost academic and social-emotional results.* Denver, CO: McREL International. Accessed at https://files.eric.ed.gov/fulltext/ED600576.pdf on March 22, 2024.

Ainsworth, L., & Donovan, K. (2019). *Rigorous curriculum design: How to create curricular units of study that align standards, instruction, and assessment* (2nd ed.). Rexford, NY: International Center for Leadership in Education.

Avanti. (2023, May 26). *The benefits of direct instruction for students with learning disabilities.* Accessed at www.my-avanti.com/the-benefits-of-direct-instruction-for-students-with-learning-disabilities on December 8, 2023.

Baepler, P., Brooks, D. C., & Walker, J. D. (Eds.). (2014). *Active learning spaces: New directions for teaching and learning.* San Francisco: Jossey-Bass.

Benson, K. (2017, October 4). *The magic relationship ratio, according to science* [Blog post]. Accessed at www.gottman.com/blog/the-magic-relationship-ratio-according-science on October 28, 2023.

Bjork, E. L., & Bjork, R. A. (2014). Making things hard on yourself, but in a good way: Creating desirable difficulties to enhance learning. In M. A. Gernsbacher & J. R. Pomerantz (Eds.), *Psychology and the real world: Essays illustrating fundamental contributions to society* (2nd ed., pp. 59–68). New York: Worth.

Bjork Learning and Forgetting Lab. (n.d.). *Applying cognitive psychology to enhance educational practice.* Accessed at https://bjorklab.psych.ucla.edu/research on July 12, 2024.

Blackburn, B. (2018). Productive struggle is a learner's sweet spot. *ASCD Express, 14*(11). Accessed at www.ascd.org/ascd-express/vol14/num11/productive-struggle-is-a-learners-sweet-spot.aspx on July 12, 2024.

Burgoyne, M. E., & Ketcham, C. J. (2015). Observation of classroom performance using therapy balls as a substitute for chairs in elementary school children. *Journal of Education and Training Studies, 3*(4), 42–48. https://doi.org/10.11114/jets.v3i4.730

CAST. (2018). *Universal Design for Learning guidelines version 2.2.* Accessed at https://udlguidelines.cast.org on March 29, 2024.

Clear, J. (n.d.). *How long does it actually take to form a new habit? (Backed by science).* Accessed at https://jamesclear.com/new-habit on October 20, 2023.

Cognitive overload. (2018, April 19). In *APA dictionary of psychology.* Accessed at https://dictionary.apa.org/cognitive-overload on October 11, 2023.

Collaboration. (n.d.). In *Oxford learner's dictionaries.* Accessed at www.oxfordlearnersdictionaries.com/us/definition/american_english/collaboration on January 23, 2024.

Collaborative for Academic, Social, and Emotional Learning. (n.d.). *What is the CASEL framework?* Accessed at https://casel.org/fundamentals-of-sel/what-is-the-casel-framework on November 14, 2023.

Common Core State Standards Initiative. (n.d.). *Read the standards.* Accessed at www.thecorestandards.org/read-the-standards on October 25, 2023.

Communication overload. (2018, April 19). In *APA dictionary of psychology.* Accessed at https://dictionary.apa.org/communication-overload on October 11, 2023.

Conzemius, A. E., & O'Neill, J. (2014). *The handbook for SMART school teams: Revitalizing best practices for collaboration* (2nd ed.). Bloomington, IN: Solution Tree Press.

Cornell University. (n.d.). *Center for Teaching Innovation: Universal design for learning.* Accessed at https://teaching.cornell.edu/teaching-resources/designing-your-course/universal-design-learning on October 14, 2023.

Covey, S. (2014). *The 7 habits of highly effective teens: The ultimate teenage success guide.* New York: Simon & Schuster.

Dondi, M., Klier, J., Panier, F., & Schubert, J. (2021, June 25). *Defining the skills citizens will need in the future world of work.* Accessed at www.mckinsey.com/industries/public-sector/our-insights/defining-the-skills-citizens-will-need-in-the-future-world-of-work on September 30, 2023.

Duckworth, A. (2016). *Grit: The power of passion and perseverance.* New York: Scribner.

Dwyer, T., Sallis, J. F., Blizzard, L., Lazarus, R., & Dean, K. (2001). Relation of academic performance to physical activity and fitness in children. *Pediatric Exercise Science, 13*(3), 225–237. https://doi.org/10.1123/pes.13.3.225

Fisher, D., Frey, N., & Hattie, J. A. C. (2016). *Visible learning for literacy, grades K–12: Implementing the practices that work best to accelerate student learning.* Thousand Oaks, CA: Corwin Press.

Fredricks, J. A. (2014). *Eight myths of student disengagement: Creating classrooms of deep learning.* Thousand Oaks, CA: Corwin Press.

Gettinger, M., & Seibert, J. K. (2002). Best practices in increasing academic learning time. In A. Thomas & J. Grimes (Eds.), *Best practices in school psychology IV* (pp. 773–787). Bethesda, MD: National Association of School Psychologists.

Goodwin, B., & Rouleau, K. (2022). *The new classroom instruction that works: The best research-based strategies for increasing student achievement.* Arlington, VA: ASCD.

Hardin, C. L. (2017). *Flexible seating in the early childhood classroom* [Master's thesis, Northwestern College]. NWCommons. https://nwcommons.nwciowa.edu/cgi/viewcontent.cgi?article=1050&context=education_masters

Hargreaves, A. (2021). The future of learning lies in engagement. *Educational Leadership, 79*(4), 26–31.

Hattie, J. A. C. (2009). *Visible learning: A synthesis of over 800 meta-analyses relating to achievement.* New York: Routledge.

Hattie, J. A. C. (2015, October 27). *Hattie ranking: 252 influences and effect sizes related to student achievement.* Accessed at https://visible-learning.org/hattie-ranking-influences-effect-sizes-learning-achievement on October 28, 2023.

Hattie, J. A. C. (2021). What can we learn from COVID-era instruction? *Educational Leadership, 78*(8).

Hattie, J. A. C. (2023). *Visible learning: The sequel—A synthesis of over 2,100 meta-analyses relating to achievement.* New York: Routledge.

Hira, A., & Anderson, E. (2021). Motivating online learning through project-based learning during the 2020 COVID-19 pandemic. *IAFOR Journal of Education, 9*(2), 93–110. https://doi.org/10.22492/ije.9.2.06

Holmes, B. (2024, July 4). *6 powerful strategies to foster student accountability*. Accessed at www.schoolplanner.com/6-powerful-strategies-foster-student-accountability on July 29, 2024.

Horn, M. B., & Staker, H. (2015). *Blended: Using disruptive innovation to improve schools*. San Francisco: Jossey-Bass.

Illustrative Mathematics. (2021). *Grade 2, unit 4, lesson 7: Addition and subtraction on the number line*. Menlo Park, CA: Open Up Resources. Accessed at https://access.openupresources.org/curricula/our-k5-math/en/grade-2/unit-4/section-b/lesson-7/student.html on March 22, 2024.

Johnson, D. W., & Johnson, R. T. (1996). Peacemakers: Teaching students to resolve their own and schoolmates' conflicts. *Focus on Exceptional Children, 28*(6). Accessed at https://journals.ku.edu/focusXchild/article/view/6855/6207 on August 19, 2024.

Johnson, D. W., Johnson, R. T., & Smith, K. A. (2014). Cooperative learning: Improving university instruction by basing practice on validated theory. *Journal on Excellence in College Teaching, 25*(3–4), 85–118.

Jones, F., & Jones, P. (2023). *Tools for teaching: Discipline, instruction, motivation—The critical skills of classroom management* (4th ed.). Santa Cruz, CA: Fredric H. Jones & Associates.

Kaman, S., & Ertem, I. S. (2018). The effect of digital texts on primary students' comprehension, fluency, and attitude. *Eurasian Journal of Educational Research, 76*, 147–164.

Kaufman, T. (n.d.). *Building positive relationships with students: What brain science says*. Accessed at www.understood.org/en/articles/brain-science-says-4-reasons-to-build-positive-relationships-with-students on October 28, 2023.

Kenyatta, A. (2020). Student responsibility: Holding oneself accountable. *Journal of Social and Emotional Learning, 1*(9), 16–17.

Kenyatta, A., & Cornecelli, E. (2020). The ins and outs of goal-setting. *Journal of Social and Emotional Learning, 1*(9), 6–7.

Kise, J. A. G. (2021). *Doable differentiation: Twelve strategies to meet the needs of all learners*. Bloomington, IN: Solution Tree Press.

Knight, S. (2017, June 13). *Brain engagement: A look at chemical reactions in the classroom* [Blog post]. Accessed at www.gcu.edu/blog/teaching-school-administration/brain-engagement-look-chemical-reactions-classroom on October 1, 2023.

Kraft, M. A. (2020). The hidden cost of classroom interruptions. *Educational Leadership, 77*(9), 33–37.

Krueger, N. (2022, October 5). *5 reasons why it is more important than ever to teach creativity* [Blog post]. Accessed at https://iste.org/blog/5-reasons-why-it-is-more-important-than-ever-to-teach-creativity on March 22, 2024.

Learning-Styles-Online.com. (2017). *Overview of learning styles.* Accessed at www.learning-styles-online.com/overview on March 22, 2024.

Lei, H., Cui, Y., & Zhou, W. (2018). Relationships between student engagement and academic achievement: A meta-analysis. *Social Behavior and Personality: An International Journal, 46*(3), 517–528. https://doi.org/10.2224/sbp.7054

Lesley University. (n.d.). *STEAM learning in action.* Accessed at https://lesley.edu/article/steam-learning-in-action on March 22, 2024.

Liljedahl, P. (2021). *Building thinking classrooms in mathematics, grades K–12: 14 teaching practices for enhancing learning.* Thousand Oaks, CA: Corwin Mathematics.

Many, T. W., & Horrell, T. (2022). *Prioritizing the standards using R.E.A.L. criteria* [Reproducible]. Accessed at https://cloudfront-s3.solutiontree.com/pdfs/Reproducibles_EYT/prioritizingthestandardsusingrealcriteria.pdf on July 1, 2024.

Marzano, R. J. (2016). *The Marzano compendium of instructional strategies.* Centennial, CO: Marzano Resources.

Marzano, R. J. (2019). *The handbook for the new art and science of teaching.* Bloomington, IN: Solution Tree Press.

Marzano, R. J., Pickering, D. J., & Pollock, J. E. (2001). *Classroom instruction that works: Research-based strategies for increasing student achievement.* Arlington, VA: ASCD.

Marzano, R. J., Warrick, P., & Simms, J. A. (2014). *A handbook for High Reliability Schools: The next step in school reform.* Bloomington, IN: Marzano Resources.

Mattos, M., Buffum, A., Malone, J., Cruz, L. F., Dimich, N., & Schuhl, S. (2025). *Taking action: A handbook for RTI at Work* (2nd ed.). Bloomington, IN: Solution Tree Press.

Meador, D. (2019, July 1). *Basic strategies for providing structure in the classroom.* Accessed at www.thoughtco.com/strategies-for-structure-in-the-classroom-4169394 on November 13, 2023.

Medina, J. (2014). *Brain rules: 12 principles for surviving and thriving at work, home, and school* (Updated and expanded ed.). Seattle, WA: Pear Press.

Merritt, J. M. (2014). Alternative seating for young children: Effects on learning. *American International Journal of Contemporary Research, 4*(1), 12–18.

Miller, A. (2020, July 13). *Strategies for improving small group instruction.* Accessed at www.edutopia.org/article/strategies-improving-small-group-instruction on December 1, 2020.

Moon, A. L., Wold, C. M., & Francom, G. M. (2017). Enhancing reading comprehension with student-centered iPad applications. *TechTrends: Linking Research and Practice to Improve Learning, 61*(2), 187–194.

Morrison, V., Novak, S., & Vanderwerff, T. (2019). *Infusing technology in the K–5 classroom: A guide to meeting today's academic standards* (1st ed.). Portland, OR: International Society for Technology in Education.

National Center for Education Statistics. (2022, May 31). *Roughly half of public schools report that they can effectively provide mental health services to all students in need.* Accessed at https://nces.ed.gov/whatsnew/press_releases/05_31_2022_2.asp on May 28, 2024.

National Center on Safe Supportive Learning Environments. (2023). *Relationships.* Accessed at https://safesupportivelearning.ed.gov/topic-research/engagement/relationships on November 9, 2023.

National Governors Association Center for Best Practices & Council of Chief State School Officers. (2010a). *Common Core State Standards for English language arts and literacy in history/social studies, science, and technical subjects.* Washington, DC: Authors. Accessed at https://learning.ccsso.org/wp-content/uploads/2022/11/ELA_Standards1.pdf on July 29, 2024.

National Governors Association Center for Best Practices & Council of Chief State School Officers. (2010b). *Common Core State Standards for mathematics.* Washington, DC: Authors. Accessed at https://learning.ccsso.org/wp-content/uploads/2022/11/Math_Standards1.pdf on July 29, 2024.

Núñez, J. L., & León, J. (2015). Autonomy support in the classroom: A review from self-determination theory. *European Psychologist, 20*(4), 275–283. https://doi.org/10.1027/1016-9040/a000234

Peart, N. (2019, September 10). The 12 most important skills you need to succeed at work. *Forbes.* Accessed at www.forbes.com/sites/nataliapeart/2019/09/10/the-12-most-important-skills-you-need-to-succeed-at-work on March 29, 2024.

Pepper Rollins, S. (2014). *Learning in the fast lane: 8 ways to put ALL students on the road to academic success.* Arlington, VA: ASCD.

Provenzano, N. (2023, July 13). *Lifting student engagement through smart tech use* [Blog post]. Accessed at https://iste.org/blog/lifting-student-engagement-through-smart-tech-use on March 29, 2024.

Rapp, W. H., Arndt, K. L., & Hildenbrand, S. M. (2019). *Picture inclusion! Snapshots of successful diverse classrooms.* Baltimore: Brookes.

Renaissance Learning. (2023). *What is student agency?* Accessed at www.renaissance.com/edword/student-agency on November 14, 2023.

Seppälä, E. (2014, May 8). *Connectedness and health: The science of social connection.* Accessed at https://ccare.stanford.edu/uncategorized/connectedness-health-the-science-of-social-connection-infographic on October 11, 2023.

Shabani, K., Khatib, M., & Ebadi, S. (2010). Vygotsky's zone of proximal development: Instructional implications and teachers' professional development. *English Language Teaching, 3*(4), 237–248. Accessed at https://files.eric.ed.gov/fulltext/EJ1081990.pdf on July 12, 2024.

Sheninger, E. (2021). *Disruptive thinking in our classrooms: Preparing learners for their future.* Chicago: ConnectEDD.

Sheninger, E., & Murray, T. C. (2017). *Learning transformed: 8 keys to designing tomorrow's schools, today.* Arlington, VA: ASCD.

Simms, J. A. (2025). *Where learning happens: Leveraging working memory and attention in the classroom.* Bloomington, IN: Marzano Resources.

Sousa, D. A. (2022). *How the brain learns* (6th ed.). Thousand Oaks, CA: Corwin Press.

Spencer, J., & Juliani, A. J. (2017). *Empower: What happens when students own their learning.* San Diego, CA: IMPress.

Sriram, R. (2020, April 13). *The neuroscience behind productive struggle.* Accessed at www.edutopia.org/article/neuroscience-behind-productive-struggle on September 8, 2021.

Stapp, A. C. (2019). Reconceptualizing the learning space through flexible seating: A qualitative analysis of select third-grade students' and teacher perceptions. *Research in the Schools, 26*(2), 32–44.

Stevenson University. (2023). *The importance of effective communication*. Accessed at www.stevenson.edu/online/about-us/news/importance-effective-communication on October 20, 2023.

Strathmann, C. (n.d.). *How to develop leadership skills as a student (advice from a college student)*. Accessed at https://xqsuperschool.org/teaching-learning/how-to-develop-leadership-skills-as-a-student on March 22, 2024.

Thompson, S. D., & Raisor, J. M. (2013). Meeting the sensory needs of young children. *YC Young Children, 68*(2), 34–43. Accessed at www.proquest.com/openview/62f72941d696529242db3e4db2631747/1?pq-origsite=gscholar&cbl=27755 on March 29, 2024.

University of Cambridge. (2016, August 9). *Positive teacher-student relationships boost good behaviour in teenagers for up to four years*. Accessed at www.cam.ac.uk/research/news/positive-teacher-student-relationships-boost-good-behaviour-in-teenagers-for-up-to-four-years on October 29, 2023.

Van Tassel, N., & Sadler, E. (Hosts). (2021, December 23). The brain science behind your students' (missing) engagement [Audio podcast episode]. In *Teaching Science in 3D*. Accessed at https://teachingsciencein3d.com/brain-science-student-engagement on October 20, 2023.

Vygotsky, L. S. (1978). *Mind in society. The development of higher psychological processes*. Cambridge, MA: Harvard University Press.

Wanasek, S. (2024, February 1). What is STEAM education? A concise guide to STEAM education in 21st century classroom [Blog post]. *ClassPoint*. Accessed at www.classpoint.io/blog/what-is-steam-education on March 29, 2024.

Wang, X. (2023, November 28). Exploring positive teacher-student relationships: The synergy of teacher mindfulness and emotional intelligence. *Frontiers in Psychology, 14*. Accessed at www.frontiersin.org/journals/psychology/articles/10.3389/fpsyg.2023.1301786 on July 19, 2024.

Watkins, C. L., & Slocum, T. A. (2003). The components of direct instruction. *Journal of Direct Instruction, 3*(2), 75–110.

White, K. (2022). *Student self-assessment: Data notebooks, portfolios, and other tools to advance learning*. Bloomington, IN: Solution Tree Press.

Zenger, J., & Folkman, J. (2013, March 15). The ideal praise-to-criticism ratio. *Harvard Business Review*. Accessed at https://hbr.org/2013/03/the-ideal-praise-to-criticism on October 20, 2023.

Zhong, Q. (2019). Design of game-based collaborative learning model. *Open Journal of Social Sciences*, *7*(7). Accessed at www.scirp.org/journal/paperinformation?paperid=94042 on March 29, 2024.

Zimmerman, B. J. (2002). Becoming a self-regulated learner: An overview. *Theory Into Practice*, *41*(2), 64–70. https://doi.org/10.1207/s15430421tip4102_2

Index

NUMBERS

7 Habits of Highly Effective Teens, The (Covey), 17

A

ability grouping, 79. *See also* groups and grouping
academic conversations, 47–48
accountability. *See also* communication, accountability, and relationships
   about, 26–27
   accountability buddies, 31–32
   accountable talk, 48
   Brain, Buddy, Buddy strategy and, 33–35
   goal reflection conversation for, 32–33
   implementing accountable practices, 28–37
   understanding accountability, 27–28
achievement of mastery, benefits of, 97
Ainsworth, L., 25
American Psychological Association, 18
artificial intelligence (AI), 87
assessments
   differentiation and, 106
   digital activities and, 130
   independent activities and, 99
   self-assessment, 4, 43, 80, 96, 99, 103
Avanti Team, The, 76

B

behavior, clear behavior expectations, 19–24

Brain, Buddy, Buddy strategy
  about, 33–35
  implementation guide, 143
  independent work stations and, 95
  literacy Check, Check, Done! checklist with, 62–63
building blocks, 47
Building Thinking Classrooms in Mathematics, Grades K-12 (Liljedahl), 81

C

Center for Teaching Innovation, 8
Check, Check, Done! checklists
  example visual to help students follow small-group procedures, 22–23
  implementation guide, 143
  independent activities and, 106
  literacy Check, Check, Done! checklist with Brain, Buddy, Buddy, 62–63
  Oregon Trail Check, Check, Done! checklist, 120–121
  for planning stations, 136–137
  practice unit for kindergarten through second grade, 147–148
  practice unit for third grade through fifth grade, 151–152
  reproducible for, 153
  self-management and student agency and, 62–64
  student-engaged framework and, 7, 66–67
class meetings, 40–41
classroom discussions, 41, 76, 77
cleanup procedures, example visual for, 21
Clear, J., 24
coding and programming, 132
cognitive overload, 18
collaboration rubric example, 37

collaboration stations
  about, 110
  collaboration station activity planning template, 118
  conclusion, 121–122
  implementation guide, 144, 145, 146
  implementing collaborative activities, 115–121
  personalization of the four stations, 59
  scenario for, 109–110
  student-engaged framework and, 5, 6
  teacher self-awareness check for, 110–111
  understanding the collaboration station, 112–115
Collaborative for Academic, Social, and Emotional Learning (CASEL), 60
collaborative implementation and digital activities, 134–135
collaborative projects, 133
coloring, 47
Common Core State Standards Initiative, 26
communication
  about, 16–17
  academic conversations, 47–48
  communication overload, 18
  conversation partners, 42–45, 143
  conversation stems and prompts, 48
  implementing effective communication, 18–26
  understanding how communication breaks down, 17–18
communication, accountability, and relationships
  about, 14
  conclusion, 48
  role of accountability, 26–37
  role of communication, 16–26
  role of relationships, 38–48
  scenario for, 14

teacher self-awareness check for, 14–15
conflict
    collaboration rubric and, 37
    foundation work and, 116–117
    school relationships and, 39
    team leaders and, 36
conversation partners, 42–45, 143
conversation stems and prompts, 48
Covey, S., 17
creative projects, 99
critical-thinking tasks, 101

D

daily schedules, 24
desirable difficulty, 95
diagram labeling, 99
differentiation
    assessments and, 106
    choice and, 52, 112
    digital content stations and, 6
    minilessons and, 6, 75, 76, 78
    planning for grouping and minilesson instruction, 82–87
digital content stations
    about, 124
    conclusion, 135–137
    digital content tech tool planning template, 137
    example digital content station planning document, 130–131
    implementation guide, 144, 145, 146
    implementing digital activities, 129–135
    personalization of the four stations, 59
    scenario for, 123–124
    student-engaged framework and, 5, 6–7
    teacher self-awareness check for, 124–126
    understanding the digital content station, 126–129
digital portfolios, 133

digital storytelling, 132
direct instruction, 74, 77
disagreement charts, 117, 143
Disruptive Thinking in Our Classrooms: Preparing Learners for Their Future (Sheninger), 2, 128
Donovan, K., 25

E

educational games, 131–132
emotional bank accounts, 17
empowerment, 3–4
engagement
    digital content stations and, 127–128
    student-engaged framework, 4–8
    why we need engagement in the classroom, 3–4
English learners, 7, 106
executive function, 52
expectations
    clear behavior expectations, 19–24
    clear learning expectations, 24–26
    communication and, 16
    visuals to communicate, 20

F

factual era, 2
feedback
    effect size of, 28
    goals and, 29
    providing, 78, 102–106
Fisher, D., 16, 48, 96, 97
flexible groupings, 80–81.
    See also groups and grouping
flexible seating, 53, 55–59
Folkman, J., 17
foundation work, building the foundation, 116–117

Fredricks, J., 134
Frey, N., 16

G

game-based collaboration, 115
goals
    goal reflection conversation for accountability, 32–33
    setting independent goals, 100–101
    student goal setting, 28–33
Goodwin, B., 99
graphic organizers
    beginning, middle, and end and Venn diagram graphic organizers, 85–86
    feedback and, 104–105
    graphic organizer designed to collect data on student understanding of a literacy standard, 105
    minilessons and, 76, 78, 82
    plot chart graphic organizer, 83
    scaffolding and, 75
    stoplight and compare and contrast graphic organizers, 84–85
groups and grouping. *See also specific types of groups*
    determining group structures, 79–81
    planning for grouping and minilesson instruction, 81–87

H

habits, 24, 27
Hardin, C., 53
Hargreaves, A., 97
Hattie, J., 5, 16, 19
heterogeneous groups, 79–80. *See also* groups and grouping
Holmes, B., 27
homogeneous groups, 79. *See also* groups and grouping

Horrell, T., 25

I

implementation guide, 141–146
independent implementation and digital activities, 131–134
independent work stations
    about, 92
    conclusion, 107
    implementation guide, 144, 145, 146
    implementing independent activities, 98–106
    personalization of the four stations, 59
    scenario for, 91–92
    student-engaged framework and, 5, 6
    teacher self-awareness check for, 92–94
    understanding the independent work stations, 94–98
Infusing Technology in the K-5 Classroom (Morrison, Novak, and Vanderwerff), 126
inquiry-based learning, 113–114
interventions, 5, 75, 79, 87
introduction
    engagement, importance of, 2
    scenario for classrooms in motion, 1
    student-engaged framework, 4–8
    what you will learn in this book, 8–10
    why we need engagement in the classroom, 3–4

J

Johnson, D., 116
Johnson, R., 116

K

Kaufman, T., 39
Kenyatta, A., 27

Index

Kraft, M., 17
Krueger, N., 128

L

learner portfolios, 41–43
learning objectives, 95, 130
learning paths, providing clear, 98–100
learning stations. *See also specific stations*
    personalization of the four stations, 59–60
    visuals to post at designated learning stations, 57
    what you will learn in this book, 9–10
learning targets, 16, 26, 29, 100, 101
Lesley University, 128
Liljedahl, P., 81

M

Many, T., 25
Marzano, R., 29, 38, 41, 94, 97
Meador, D., 27
metacognition, 102–103
Miller, A., 80
minilesson stations
    about, 72
    conclusion, 89
    implementation guide, 144, 145, 146
    implementing, 77–87
    minilesson planning template, 88
    personalization of the four stations, 59
    planning for grouping and minilesson instruction, 81–87
    scenario for, 71–72
    student-engaged framework and, 5–6
    teacher self-awareness check for, 73–74
    understanding the minilesson station, 74–77
minilessons, characteristics of, 74–75

morning start-up procedures, example visual for, 21
Morrison, V., 126, 127
motivation, 52, 53
movement, 3, 54
Murray, T., 3

N

National Center for Education Statistics, 4
National Center on Safe Supportive Learning Environments, 39
New Classroom Instruction That Works, The (Goodwin and Rouleau), 99
Novak, S., 126

O

Oregon Trail Check, Check, Done! checklist, 120–121
overlearning, 96

P

partners, conversation partners, 42–45
peer reviews, 102–103
Pepper Rollins, S., 95, 98, 103
personalization and digital content stations, 129
personalized learning environments
    about, 52–53
    implementing, 55–60
    importance of, 53–54
    personalization of the four stations, 59–60
personalized learning tools
    about, 50
    conclusion, 66
    personalized learning environments, 52–60
    scenario for, 49

self-management and student
    agency, 60–66
teacher self-awareness check for, 50–51
Pickering, D., 29
Play-Doh™, 45, 47
Pollock, J., 29
practice unit for kindergarten through
    second grade, 147–150
practice unit for third grade through fifth
    grade, 151–152
problem- and inquiry-based
    learning, 113–114
problem-solving tasks, 101
productive struggle, 95
progression boards, 65–66
project-based learning, 114–115

R

random groupings, 80. *See also* groups and
    grouping
reading supports, 106
R.E.A.L. criteria, 25. *See also* standards
real-world learning and creativity, 128–129
reflection
    accountability and, 31, 32, 33
    effect size of, 28
    feedback and, 103
    implementing digital activities and, 130
    learner portfolios and, 43
    learning targets and, 29, 101
relationships. *See also* communication,
        accountability, and relationships
    about, 38
    engagement and, 4
    implementing practices for positive
        relationships, 39–48
    understanding school relationships, 39
relevance, 95–96, 101–102

reproducible for Check, Check, Done!
    checklist, 153
research projects, 101
research tasks, 99
Rouleau, K., 99

S

scaffolding
    conversation stems and prompts and, 48
    independent work stations and, 96
    minilessons and, 75, 78
    planning for grouping and minilesson
        instruction, 82–87
schedules, example visual of daily
    schedule, 24
self-assessment, 4, 43, 80, 96, 99, 103.
    See also assessments
self-efficacy, 19, 28
self-management and student agency
    about, 60–61
    implementing practices for self-
        management and student
        agency, 61–66
    understanding self-management and
        student agency, 61
sensory stimulation, 54
Seppälä, E., 38
Sheninger, E., 2, 3, 60, 61, 101, 128
Slocum, T., 77
small groups. *See also* groups and grouping
    direct instruction and, 101
    example visual to help students follow
        small-group procedures, 22–23
    interventions and, 79
    minilessons and, 75, 76, 77
SMART goals, 29. *See also* goals
soft starts, 45–47, 143
Sriram, R., 96
stability balls, use of, 54

Index

standards, 25–26, 81
Stevenson University, 16
storytelling, 132
student agency, definition of, 60. *See also* self-management and student agency
student learner profile example, 41–42
student-engaged framework and, 4–8
success criteria, 96

T

tangrams, 47
team leaders, 36–37
time management, 35

U

Universal Design for Learning (UDL), 8, 129
University of Cambridge, 39

V

Vanderwerff, T., 126
visuals
　example visual of the daily schedule on students' desks, 24
　example visual to help students follow a cleanup procedure, 21
　example visual to help students follow a morning start-up procedure, 21
　example visual to help students follow small-group procedures, 22–23
　visuals to communicate expectations, 20, 24
　visuals to post at designated learning stations, 57

W

Wanasek, S., 113
Watkins, C., 77
whole-group instruction, 19, 101. *See also* groups and grouping

Z

Zenger, J., 17
Zhong, Q., 115
zone of proximal development (ZPD), 95

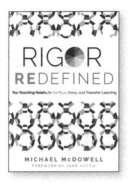

Rigor Redefined
Michael McDowell

Teachers can use Michael McDowell's ten learning habits, practical tools, and templates to actualize rigorous instruction in short and sharp ways that drive student learning and create a lasting impact. Discover how to connect the dots between surface, deep, and transfer learning.
BKG193

The Digital Projects Playbook
John Arthur

Students in today's classrooms live in a digital world. Tap into the unique opportunities this offers with author John Arthur's collection of resource-packed projects designed to leverage students' digital skills and support their academic, cognitive, and creative development.
BKG171

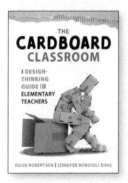

The Cardboard Classroom
Doug Robertson with Jennifer Borgioli Binis

In *The Cardboard Classroom*, authors Doug Robertson and Jennifer Borgioli Binis offer practical guidance and sample projects developed from Robertson's authentic classroom experiences to help you find space for this engaging approach to instruction in your daily practice.
BKG023

Teach Brilliantly
James A. Nottingham

Identify the quick instructional wins that will help every student be successful. This in-depth action guide by James A. Nottingham, creator of the renowned teaching model the Learning Pit, distills cutting-edge research and best practices from classrooms worldwide into one indispensable teacher toolbox.
BKG198

Solution Tree | Press

Visit SolutionTree.com or call 800.733.6786 to order.

"Excellent engagement in what truly matters in **assessment**.

Great examples!"

—Carol Johnson, superintendent,
Central Dauphin School District, Pennsylvania

PD Services

Our experts draw from decades of research and their own experiences to bring you practical strategies for designing and implementing quality assessments. You can choose from a range of customizable services, from a one-day overview to a multiyear process.

Book your assessment PD today!
888.763.9045

Solution Tree